Tricks of the Nintendo® Masters

Ed Tiley

HAYDEN BOOKS

A Division of Howard W. Sams & Company

11711 North College, Suite 141, Carmel, IN 46032 USA

FIRST EDITION
FIRST PRINTING—1990

International Standard Book Number: 0-672-48482-X
Library of Congress Catalog Card Number: 90-70470

Contributing Author: *Allen Wyatt*
Acquisitions Editor: *Marie Butler-Knight*
Manuscript Editor: *Joe Kraynak*
Production Coordinator: *Becky Imel*
Designer: *Glenn Santner*
Cover Artist: *Ned Shaw*
Production: *Brad Chinn, Sally Copenhaver,
Tami Hughes, William Hurley, Charles Hutchinson,
Jodi Jensen, Lori Lyons, Jennifer Matthews,
Dennis Sheehan, Joe Ramon, Mary Beth Wakefield*

Printed in the United States of America

To the memory of my great-grandparents, Perley A. and Margaret Thomas. Together they raised a family, built the streetcar named "Desire" and made school buses safer for generations of children.

Their life's work—continued by their children—has made a better world for their descendants and touched the lives of millions.

Contents

Arcade Titles, *27*

Action/Adventure Titles, *61*

Military Games, *135*

Quizzlers, *167*

Role-Playing Games, *191*

Sports Simulations, *209*

Hot Controllers, *261*

GameBoy, *269*

Introducing the Testers

The tips and strategies in this book come from young players themselves. In addition to my own four children, we had a crew of terrific Nintendo players who shared their experiences and tricks with all of us. Some of these kids are amazing! They can take a game and master it in a matter of days! This was a big help when it came to including games that haven't been released yet.

The parents of our testers deserve a big thank-you for their cooperation as well.

Here's a photo of our testing crew:

Tester photo

Top row (left to right): *Ed Tiley, Wil Tiley, Lou Tiley, Trey Roberts, Jason Hawkins, Jason Snead.*

Bottom row: *Nicholas Taylor, Marlene Tiley, Amara Tiley, Deric Roberts, Scott Hornsby, Dylan Tiley.*

Kneeling: *Kirk Reams, Kevin Hornsby.*

Lying at the master's feet is *Goldie.*

Not pictured: *Blair Graham, Kristan Donohue, Brent Satterfield, Ryan Satterfield, Ryan Pasco, Richard Corsale, Todd Bodziony, Joe Wyrick, and Mike Maddux.*

Photo credit: *Bob O'Lary.*

Introduction

At first glance, the Nintendo system doesn't look like a wildfire. Outwardly it is a simple gray box with two rectangular controllers that plug into the front panel. A power connection and a plug that hooks onto the TV set complete the basic system. But insert a game cartridge into the hinged compartment of the NES, and the fun begins!

Suddenly the world is transformed into a fantasy land of ninjas, evil wizards, super cars, deadly monsters, and space aliens. You strap on the armor and lift the weapon of the avenging hero to begin your quest and defeat the evil demons . . . all in the comfort of your home.

About This Book

The neat thing about video games is that each one contains hidden surprises. You press a certain combination of keys, and you see a whole new aspect of a game. The problem is that few of these secrets are documented. One of the programmers who designed the game may have sneaked them in at the last minute—after the instruction booklet was written.

To get around this problem, kids have traditionally resorted to hanging around playgrounds and trading secrets. There's always one kid who seems to be able to make the game do whatever he wants by using secret passwords and little tricks.

The purpose of this book is to let you in on some of the secrets and reveal some of the passwords, so you can get the most out of the game. We're not giving away any endings, though. You'll still have to search and experiment to master these games, and you'll still have the feeling you get from doing it on your own. But the tips included here will give you a start.

The Breakdown

This book contains information about more than sixty different games. The listings are arranged alphabetically within the following categories:

Titles
for Tots — The games in this section appeal mostly to younger players, but the entire family may get a kick out of some of these games.

Arcade — Many of the games in this category first appeared in the coin-operated arcade machines. Others are so similar to these arcade classics that you'll want to shove quarters into the front of your Nintendo system.

Action/
Adventure — These games provide you with a character, a goal, and a set path for achieving the goal. Usually, you need to fight your way through several levels, each level being harder than the one before. To win, you must complete each level and then do battle with the main villain of the game.

Military — These games let you test yourself in all sorts of combat situations. Most of these games resemble action/adventure titles except that the enemies are usually human and the weapons tend to be a little less futuristic.

Quizzlers — This group of games includes puzzles, mind benders, and Nintendo versions of popular TV quiz shows.

Role-Playing
Games — These games give you a character and a goal, but no set path for achieving the goal. Instead, you must find items and locate treasures to strengthen your character and make you ready for the finale. Instead of progressing through levels, you must move through a mythical land, usually at your own pace.

Sports — These games simulate athletic competition in almost every major sport.

Even though the games covered in this book are arranged according to these categories, keep in mind that few games are so completely predictable as to fall into just one category. An action game will also have elements of role playing, or an arcade game may combine military situations with science fiction or magic.

The Game Listings

Space limitations prevent us from listing every game available for the Nintendo system, but we've included the most popular games. You should be able to go down to your local store and find most (if not all) of the games listed.

These listings are not reviews! All of the games were selected because of their play value or wide audience. You can use the listings to see if the content of a game is interesting to you, but this book is not meant to be a buyer's guide. One of the best ways to find out if you would like to own a particular game is to rent it for a day or two at your local video store.

Getting into the Action

Once you find the game you want to learn about, you'll notice that the game coverage is broken down into the following four sections:

Up Front	This section describes the game. If the game has a plot, we describe the plot to give you some idea of what to expect when you start out.
Getting Started	This section describes the basics. You will find information about using the controller, selecting options, and collecting power-ups, as well as other information that you need to know to get a fast start.
Moving On	In this section you will find information that will help you become familiar with the game. This section will contain detailed strategies to get you through the first part of the game.

| Master Tips | This section of the listing will tell you about secret continues, hidden features, and strategies for doing well in later stages of the game. |

 Look for the power-up icon as shown at the left for a list of items that will give you strength, wisdom, life, and (most importantly) weapons.

Acknowledgments

Special thanks to the following companies who generously contributed the color screen shots for this book: Acclaim Entertainment, Activision, CSG Imagesoft, High Tech Expressions, Hudson Soft, Jaleco USA, Konami Industry, LJN Toys, Milton Bradley, and Ultra Software.

Trademarks

All terms mentioned in this book
that are known to be trademarks or
service marks are listed below. In
addition, terms suspected of being
trademarks or service marks have
been appropriately capitalized.
Howard W. Sams & Company
cannot attest to the accuracy of this
information. Use of a term in this
book should not be regarded as
affecting the validity of any
trademark or service mark.

Bugs Bunny's Crazy Castle (Seika)
Sesame Street 123 and Sesame
  Street ABC (Hi-Tech
  Expressions)
Shooting Range (Bandai)
RoadBlasters and Paperboy
  (Mindscape)
RoboCop, Bad Dudes and Rampage
  (®Data East USA, Inc.)
A Boy and His Blob (Absolute)
Blaster Master (®Sun Corporation of
  America)
Fester's Quest (Sunsoft)
Gauntlet and Pac-Man (®Tengen)
River City Ransom and Double
  Dragon (®Technos Japan Corp.,
  Tradewest, Inc.)
Skate or Die (®Ultra Software
  Corporation)
The Uncanny X-men, Back to the
  Future, and Who Framed Roger
  Rabbit? (LJN Toys, Ltd.)
Stealth ATF (Activision, Inc.)
Hollywood Squares, Jeopardy, and
  Wheel of Fortune (Game Tek)
Tetris (™V/O Electronorgtechnica)
Willow, Strider, 1943, Duck Tales,
  Mega Man 2 and Bionic
  Commando (®Capcom USA, Inc.)
Baseball Simulator 1.000 (Culture
  Brain)
Hoops, Bases Loaded II Second
  Season, and Astyanax (®Jaleco
  USA Inc.)

Jordan vs. Bird: One on One and
  Marble Madness (®Milton Bradley
  Company)
Lee Trevino's Fighting Golf and Iron
  Tank (®SNK Electronics
  Corporation of America)
Mike Tyson's Punch-Out, Excitebike,
  Zelda II: The Adventures of Link,
  Dragon Warrior, Anticipation,
  Super Mario Bros. 2, Super
  Mario Bros. 3, and Nintendo
  (®Nintendo of America, Inc.)
Super Mario Land, GameBoy,
  Alleyway, and Kid Icarus
  (™Nintendo of America, Inc.)
Super Dodge Ball (CSG Imagesoft)
Tecmo Bowl and Ninja Gaiden
  (®Tecmo, Inc.)
Camerica (Camerica)
Toycard SSS, Bomberman, Xexyz,
  Adventures of Dino Riki (Hudson
  Soft USA, Inc.)
Double Player and Ironsword:
  Wizards and Warriors II
  (®Acclaim Entertainment, Inc.)
Zoomer (Beeshu)
Blades of Steel, Double Dribble,
  Castlevania II: Simon's Quest,
  Top Gun II, The Adventures of
  Bayou Billy, Contra, Jackal,
  Metal Gear, Silent Service, and
  Life Force (®Konami Industry
  Co., Ltd.)
The Castlevania Adventure and
  Track and Field II (™Konami
  Industry Co., Ltd.)
Revenge of the 'Gator (™Hal
  America, Inc.)
Adventures of Lolo (™Hal America,
  Inc.)
Teenage Mutant Ninja Turtles
  (®Mirage Studios, USA)
Batman (™DC Comics, Inc.)

These games grab the interest of kids from ages four to seven, giving them worlds that they can fully explore and challenges that are realistic. Although older players may also find these games interesting, they can usually master the games too easily.

Titles
for Tots

Bugs Bunny's Crazy Castle

Manufacturer: *Seika*

Up Front

Sylvester, Daffy Duck, and Yosemite Sam have locked Bugs' girlfriend, Honey Bunny, in Crazy Castle—a loony maze. You're Bugs and you have to rescue her. To get Honey Bunny out of the maze, you must collect the carrots on each level, without being touched by your foes. Sound easy? Well, it is and it isn't.

    Each "room" of the castle is a maze of stairways and doors or a series of pipes that you must get through. Along the way, you'll find many items to help you—boxing gloves that you can use to flatten opponents, flower pots to drop on their heads, packing crates, ten-ton weights, and even safes that you can use to smash your wily foes.

Each maze has a number of carrots that you must snatch. For each carrot you pick up you earn points. Yosemite and the rest of his gang will try to keep you from getting to the carrots. If they succeed in touching you, you must replay that level. Each time you succeed in running the maze you're awarded a 1-up; this gives you more attempts to complete the maze.

At the end of each maze you're given a four-digit password that lets you return to a particular level at another time. The passwords, however, are pretty random, so it's hard to guess a password for any particular maze. You need to complete a level before you can get its password.

Getting Started

The game begins easily enough. The first few mazes are simple, so you can get the hang of using the controller to move Bugs around:

◀▶	Move Bugs.
▲	Climb stairs or enter pipes above Bugs. (If you can see stairs in the doorway, they go up. If you can't see stairs, they go down.)
▼	Go down stairs or pass through pipes under Bugs' feet.
Ⓐ	Throw the boxing glove.

Be careful going down stairs or through a pipe. Once Bugs starts, you can't change his direction or stop until he gets to the bottom. Don't be surprised if you meet Daffy or Sylvester at the bottom. Remember that Bugs and his buddies are toons; jumping off ledges and falling down shafts won't hurt them.

As Bugs touches a carrot, he picks it up and you earn points. Collect all the carrots without being touched to complete the level and receive a 1-up.

Along the way, you'll find stuff that you can use against your enemies. Pick up the boxing glove to punch out an opponent, removing him from the maze. Try throwing the boxing glove from a distance—don't wait till the bad guys are right in Bugs' face!

You can also attack your enemies with crates, weights, flower pots, and safes. Either drop the items on your opponent or kick them into an opponent.

But don't get rid of your weapons too quickly—save them for when you really need them. Try to avoid the enemies instead. Bugs won't be harmed when he passes Sylvester or one of the others in stairways or pipes, so that's one good way of avoiding them. Another good way is to run past the foe. Remember, Bugs is a bunny, and like all bunnies, he's quick! Whenever the coast is clear, make a break for it.

Moving On

Some mazes have two boxing gloves. Pick up both of them and hang on to them till you're in a jam. If you throw the glove and miss, you can pick it up and reuse it.

Along the way you will find jugs of magic potion marked XXX. When Bugs collects the jug, he becomes invincible for a few seconds. He can take out a bad guy just by touching him.

The first really hard maze is level 23. To get through this one go to the top (don't forget to collect carrots!). You have to outwit Sylvester a couple of times—duck into doorways to get by him. Come back down to where the potion is. Walk through the potion and over the ledge on the left. You're invincible now! Forget the carrot—get Daffy! Once you beat Daffy, collect the last two carrots. No hurry, Daffy's gone.

Whenever you see a no-carrot sign (a carrot in a circle with a slash across it), steer clear unless you're brave! Whenever Bugs touches a no-carrot sign, you enter a special level. If you complete the level in a single try, you get three extra "lives" (attempts), but if you're caught, you have to repeat the last three levels.

Master Tips

Here are some passwords to put you on some different levels. Next time you start the game, instead of pressing Start, choose Password, and enter the password for the level you want:

5	SXES
15	XWAS
31	XPAS
44	YZKW
51	T22X

❏ The last ten mazes are among the hardest in the game. Sure, a couple of them are easy, but the nearer your goal, the harder it gets.

❏ The trick to level 57 is to go left and grab the glove, then duck into the doorway just before Daffy gets you. Once you're on the ledge above Daffy, make sure you leap down to get the carrots at the right time. Daffy stays on the bottom, pacing back and forth. Wait until he gets past the door, then jump down for the carrot. Jump right back into the doorway and up onto the ledge. Repeat the process for the carrot on the right side. Don't get in a position where you have to use the glove on Daffy; if you do, you're a dead duck . . . er, rabbit.

❏ Once you have the carrots from the bottom of the maze, hang around on the ledge until Sylvester comes off the ledge from above and down the side to join Daffy. Tease him until he starts chasing you, then run up the stairs to the magic potion and stop. He will run right up your back and poof! You got one less cat to worry about.

Duck Tales

Manufacturer: *Capcom*

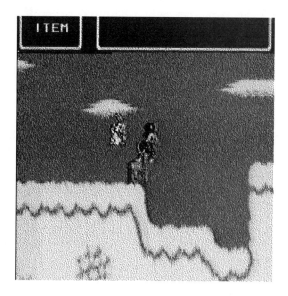

Up Front

We almost included this game in the section devoted to older players, but our seven-year-old tester showed such mastery over the game that we were convinced to put it here. That's not to say that this game is only for small children. Several teens and adults had a crack at this game and found it interesting as well.

You probably know all the characters in DuckTales. What you may not know is that millionaire Scrooge McDuck has a unique way of using his cane as a pogo stick. He doesn't just use this pogo cane to get to some out-of-the-way places, it's also his main weapon for defeating enemies.

Uncle Scrooge is on a quest to reunite five lost treasures that have been scattered across the world. He wants to bring the treasures back to the Ducksburg Museum, where the treasures will be safe. To find the treasures he must travel to the Amazon, Transylvania, through an African mine, across the Himalayas, and even to the moon! The object of the game is to collect the treasures in each land and get them back to the Control Room.

Getting Started

The first thing you have to learn in this game is the pogo jump. You'll need it right from the start. Press button A to make Scrooge jump. Before he lands press button B and hold it down. Scrooge begins bouncing. Use the arrow buttons to move around. As enemies come by, jump on 'em!

Once you can move McDuck around, you need to learn how to swing McDuck's cane as a golf club. To swing the cane, press button B when Scrooge isn't jumping. Learn to do this, and you can smash giant spiders with boulder-size golf shots, move objects, whack enemies, and crumble stones with a single stroke!

To get one of the treasures, you must make your way through a level and fight the boss of that level for the treasure. In addition to this main treasure, you can collect smaller treasures in the form of diamonds—small, large, and red diamonds. Each is increasingly more valuable. The red diamond is worth $50,000.

On each level you'll find your buddy, Launchpad. He will offer to take you back to Ducksburg with the stuff you've collected. If you choose to go back with Launchpad, you'll preserve the loot you've collected up to this point, but you'll have to begin this level all over again. (This is a good way of racking up killer point totals.)

At the top of the screen is a status area that shows the points you have scored and the money you've collected. There's also a life meter that turns from red to yellow. When all the dots are yellow, you drop off the edge of the earth.

 Look for useful items hidden in various places. Food items restore Scrooge's life meter. 1-ups and magic coins make Scrooge invulnerable for a short time. You'll find some surprises as well—I don't want to give them all away. To find these hidden items, look everywhere. Since some are invisible, they could be hiding anywhere!

Moving On

Begin your quest in the Amazon. All of our testers agree that it's a good place to start. When you select the Amazon from the Control Center, you'll find yourself standing in the middle of a jungle path. Start to pogo jump right away— a gorilla is coming!

Bounce around left and right, and time your jump so you land on things like treasure chests, stone blocks, and . . . the gorilla.

As you bounce your way around, you will begin to collect things immediately. Keep working your way to the right. You'll come to a place where there's a vine hanging down into a cave. Go there.

As you come down the vine, you'll see a statue on your left. Use the cane to move the barrel to the stone, so that you can pogo up onto the top of the statue. When you get there, bounce to the left and walk along the wall. You'll find two rooms over there, including one with invisible diamonds on the stairs.

Once you've cleaned out these rooms, come back and pogo over the spiked logs to collect a 1-up.

Always jump up into places where you wouldn't expect hidden treasures. For example, when you go past the vine that goes out of the cave, you'll see a space that dead-ends. Check it out.

There are more hidden items in the area around the vine that climbs up to the sky. Once you have these, climb up and start working your way to the left. Watch out for bees. When you get to the pillar, wait for Launchpad—he'll give you a lift to the next pillar. You'll have to jump the last little bit or the bee will get you.

Remember that you can jump higher than normal if you bounce off the back of some other creature that is flying by. Be sure to time it right!

Pogo across the bridge quickly—it begins to fall apart as soon as you touch it. Soon you will be able to get into the fortress in the air. In the upper right part of the screen is Launchpad standing on a ledge. When you approach him, he'll offer you a ride back to the Control Center. Say yes, and everything you've gotten so far will be preserved.

Jump up from where Launchpad is and get on top of the wall. There are secrets to the left.

When you come back, go down the vine and to the right. You need to time it right to get through the tunnel. If you're not careful you'll be mowed down by a big red stone. Pogo through the tunnel as quickly as you can or the nasty thing will come back and get you a second time. Keep moving to the right.

Just before the big spiders there's a hidden magic coin. Find it and you're invulnerable! Run through the next area as fast as you can. When you get all the way to the right, you will be asked for money to make the vine reachable. Don't do it! Wait for the guy who throws spears to come at you and pogo off his head up to the vine.

When you get up top and the blocks start falling, run to the left and don't stop. Use the cane to bang the barrels into the boss's room and go git him! You'll need to pogo his noggin about five times to do him in. When the boss is out of the way, a treasure chest appears containing the Scepter of the Incan King.

Next you journey to the land of Transylvania to search the haunted castle. Here you'll find piles of bones that suddenly come to life and attack you, ghosts that buzz around your head, and goblins that chase you.

Start moving to the right. Ignore the first rope you come to that goes up. Instead go all the way to the right and down a rope to the basement. Whack the suit of armor—the cake inside will restore your life meter—then start moving left. Pogo under the low wall to find six treasure chests. Once you have them all, jump over to the magic mirror and see where it takes you.

Whoops! Back to the beginning of the level. This time don't ignore the rope that leads up. Save Huey from the Beagle Boy by pogo jumping all over his head. Huey will tell you about some magic walls. Head down the rope and take the hallway to the right. At the end are secret rooms where you can find a power up. This gives your life meter an extra red ball.

On your way to the boss, you'll find a chest hanging in mid-air. Use the cane to whack a rock into it and get a 1-up.

The boss of this level is a lady duck. Forget chivalry! If you don't start pogoing her head and dodging her fire, you'll be the dead duck.

Master Tips

❏ Somewhere in Transylvania is the key that you need for the African Mines. If you don't have it when you get to the mines, you will be transported to Transylvania to get it.

❏ Jump up at the first mirror you come to and you will find yourself in a room with a chest. Bounce the chest to get the skeleton key (what else!). Jump into the mirror on the left to get back to Control Center.

❏ An illusion wall in the mines hides a 1-up—get it.

❏ Free Bubba from the ice and get another red ball for your life meter. There's a big blue hole in the ice—fall into it to take a different route through the Himalayas.

❏ Gizmo and the remote control have something to do with helping you get green cheese from the Moon Mouse.

❏ If you can't reach a place, try moving an object or keep an eye peeled for some enemy that you can pogo off.

Sesame Street 123

Manufacturer: *Hi-Tech Expressions*

Up Front

If there is one thing in this world you can count on, it's that anything with the Children's Television Workshop name will be educational and wholesome. The Sesame Street game cartridges are no exception. Rather than the usual routine of blasting hostile space aliens into oblivion, this game features the Zips—friendly aliens here to help build cities, not destroy them. Of course some stereotypes remain; they are represented as little green men!

Actually this cartridge contains two collections of games. The first is entitled Astro-Grover and features everybody's favorite furry monster in a series of counting games. When the right answers are given, the man in the moon smiles and the Zips build part of the city.

The second collection, Ernie's Magic Shapes, is a series of color and shape matching games. Ernie is a magician—he makes shapes (or groups of shapes) appear over his head. Then he makes shapes appear over his magician's top hat. If the shapes don't match, press the arrow button to change the shape. If the shapes match, press either button A or B—magic stars appear and the rabbit cheers for you.

To choose a game, use the arrows to highlight the game you want to play on the title screen. Press Reset and then press Start to start the newly selected game.

Getting Started

Each game within one of the collections builds on the previous game. The Astro-Grover series starts with a spaceship beaming Zips onto the screen. Count the Zips and use the arrow buttons to choose the answer.

Ernie's Magic Shapes starts with simple shape matching, then moves to shape and color matching and choosing pieces of patterns.

Moving On

This cartridge is definitely not a babysitter. Children get much more out of the games if an adult or older (patient) brother or sister works with them. In fact, when left to her own devices, our five-year-old tester quickly became bored. With an adult playing along, her attention span and general satisfaction with the games increased dramatically.

Master Tips

❏ Adults may find that the slow pace of this game can be tiresome. Children, however, will find that it is just the right pace. The time periods of relative inactivity allow the adult participant to expand on the basic offerings of the game by asking the child to count the Zips as they are beamed on and off the screen. Similarly the shape games allow time for discussions about the names of shapes and colors.

❏ Remember that young attention spans are short! Two or three ten-minute play periods are much more successful than coaxing the child to continue on for a full hour.

Sesame Street ABC

Manufacturer: *Hi-Tech Expressions*

Up Front

Sesame Street ABC is the second in the Children's Television Workshop series. Like the Sesame Street 123 cartridge, this cartridge contains two games—Letter-Go-Round and Ernie's Big Splash. As the name implies, Letter-Go-Round is an alphabet game. Ernie's Big Splash is a maze construction game that lets the child build a pathway for Rubber Ducky to find his way into Ernie's bathtub.

This cartridge, like its 123 counterpart, works best when parent and child play together. Four, five and six year-olds will love this cartridge.

Getting Started

The title screen of this game gives you a choice between the two different games. Use the arrow button to select the game you want to play, then press either red button.

There are six variations on Letter-Go-Round. The first three involve letter matching. Level one is all uppercase letters, level two is all lowercase letters, and level three is a mixture of uppercase and lowercase.

In each of these variations, letters are put on the ferris wheel. A matching letter is shown at the bottom of the screen, and the child must match the letter by pressing one of the red buttons as the letter gets into the matching zone located at the bottom of the wheel.

You can control how fast the wheel spins with the arrow buttons, but don't underestimate your youngster's reflexes; they're probably faster than you think. Experiment a little to learn about your child's abilities.

The fourth game in Letter-Go-Round is called One Little Word. Kids try to match the letters in the word, building their vocabulary of three letter words. In the fifth game, players must supply the missing letter in the word.

The sixth variation is the toughest, even though only three-letter words are used. In this variation, players must figure out what the secret word is from the letters available on the wheel. Sometimes there's more than one choice. Success in any level is rewarded by dancing Muppets and a fireworks show.

Moving On

In Ernie's Big Splash, children are encouraged to construct pathways to help Rubber Ducky find his way into the bathtub, where Ernie is waiting. The idea behind this game is to teach children about cause and effect. If the child builds a dead-end path, Rubber Ducky just won't be able to get to Ernie in the tub.

There are three different levels to this game. In the first level, the child can create a simple path for Rubber Ducky to travel, by piecing together blocks to form a path. Each of the possible choices lets Rubber Ducky move through the block in a certain way (for example, in through the top and out the left side). Each block has arrows that show the direction Rubber Ducky will travel.

In the second and third levels, Muppet characters are placed in boxes on the screen so you can direct the path towards them. The characters' boxes have four openings so that they can be used in the pathway twice. Of course the player always has the option to bypass the character box entirely.

In Ernie's Big Splash, we find Ernie seated in the bathtub waiting for his pal Rubber Ducky, who is located in another part of the screen. The player uses the arrow buttons to select from a series of boxes that have arrows showing the travel path. The travel path is indicated by green arrows on the screen showing, for example, that Rubber Ducky might come in the left side of the box and go out the top or bottom.

Use the arrow buttons to select a travel path, then press either red button. As the child creates travel paths for Rubber Ducky, he will move along the path toward the bathtub. If the child builds a pathway that is a dead end or wants to start over for any other reason, pressing the Start button will clear the screen for a restart. Pressing Start twice will take you back to the level selection process.

Master Tips

❏ Like its companion cartridge, Sesame Street ABC is best suited for parent-child interaction. The instruction sheet that comes with the game gives numerous constructive hints on how to make the child's playtime more meaningful by introducing the concepts of letters, words, and matching.

Shooting Range

Manufacturer: *Bandai*

Up Front

If you have a light-gun for your Nintendo system and you have a young child, you should have Shooting Range. This non-violent game will provide hours of fun for the whole family. While the older kids will play it for a change of pace, the tots in the family will probably like it enough to make it their game of choice.

What makes this game attractive to young players is its simplicity. Targets appear on the screen and you blast them.

You can compete with yourself or with up to three other players for high score.

Getting Started

To get the game going use the Start button to access the selection screens. Choose the number of players, then choose either the normal game or the party mode and the level of difficulty. In the normal game you proceed through three stages: the Old West, the Haunted House, and Outer Space. If you score well, you're given the opportunity to take on the Bonus Round.

The actual screen is about one and a half times wider than the TV screen. If there's no action on the screen, use the left and right arrows to pan across to the parts of the screen you can't see. One of our testers put the controller on the floor and pressed the arrows with his feet.

During the game you shoot at pinwheel targets (not the character holding them) as a clock counts down. The energy bar on screen winds down when you miss too many shots. When either your time or your energy is spent, the game is over. If you score enough hits, you clear the screen and get points for the time you have left over.

 Some of the targets will turn into power ups when you hit them. To collect the power up you must hit it:

Small E	Adds two bars of energy to your meter.
Large E	Completely restores your energy.
Backward E	Takes away two energy bars. Don't shoot at it and it won't hurt you. When you're shooting hot and heavy, this is easier said than done.
Circled C	100 points.
Circled W	1,000 points.
Hourglass	Gives you an additional 50 seconds.

Moving On

After the wild west, you'll find yourself on the lawn of the Haunted House. Witches, mummies, and vampires will be carrying targets for you to shoot at.

The third stage is Outer Space. In this game the targets are carried by an odd assortment of space creatures. Everything's pretty normal until the clock runs down to 99 seconds. That's when a big flying monster with a pinwheel in his mouth comes swooping across the screen. Shoot when his mouth is open. It takes several shots to do this guy in.

Remember that wasted shots deplete your energy level. The best way to get the monster is to use the arrow buttons to pan the background. This will make the monster seem like he's standing still. When the mouth opens, blast the target. If you score a hit, the monster will be stunned. Wait for him to start flying again before shooting or you will be wasting energy.

If you score well in any of the rounds, you get a chance at the bonus round before the next stage. The bonus round is slightly different—no pinwheels. Instead, you get to shoot at a shelf of bottles. When the bottles turn white, you can break them. Be patient, don't waste shots. Look for patterns in how the bottles turn colors, then time your shots.

If you get a great score, you can put your initials in the top five. Unfortunately the cartridge loses this information as soon as you take it out of the machine.

The party game consists of lights on a background and holes where pinwheel targets will pop up. Each player tries to get as many points as possible before the clock runs out.

To get shots, blast one of the lights when it's lit. You can then shoot at the targets as they pop up through the holes on sticks. If you pull the trigger and nothing happens, shoot another light to get more shots. The player with the most points wins.

Master Tips

❑ The light-gun can be a bit tricky at times. The brightness and contrast on the TV set must be set just right to make sure all the shots are registering.

❏ The way the light gun works is slick. When you pull the trigger, a white square replaces the target for just a fraction of a second (you don't really see it unless you are looking for it). If the gun is properly aimed, a sensor in the gun reads the light level change made by the white square and registers a hit. If the contrast and brightness are too high, the gun can't see the white square. If the levels are too low, almost anything registers as a hit.

❏ The optimum range for the gun is about six feet. The cord is a little longer than six feet. If you move as far away as you can without the cord pulling on you, you're at about the right distance. If you are right on top of the screen, it's too easy.

For Parents Only

If this gives you an idea of how you might give a very small uncoordinated child an edge and a feeling of success . . . just don't tell the older kids you heard it here.

Of course the kids figure this out on their own pretty quickly. Let's just say that if you get into a serious shooting competition with your teen-agers, don't let them fiddle with any dials between turns.

Who Framed Roger Rabbit?

Manufacturer: *LJN*

Up Front

Eddie Valiant and Roger set out in Los Angeles of the 1940s to discover all the clues needed to confront Judge Doom and solve the mystery surrounding the murder of Marvin Acme, the owner of ToonTown.

Along the way you'll discover a large number of hidden items, weapons, and clues. You will have to search the town from top to bottom, all the time avoiding the Weasels and other dangers. Be sure to talk to everybody you meet—they will often give you valuable information.

One of the charms of this game is that it enables young players to take on a role-playing challenge without the coordination needed to fight through hordes of nasties like in Castlevania II. Older players (9 and above) will find this game to be simple. They will beat it quickly, then lose interest.

Getting Started

There are two different views used in this game. When Roger and Eddie are moving between locations, you see the action from overhead. When they move into a building, or some other location, the view switches to a more normal side shot. In either case, use the controls to make the following moves:

⭥◀▶	Move around the screen and through doors.
Select	Choose one of the items you've found along the way.
Ⓑ	Use the chosen object or weapon.
Ⓐ	Talk to people and to search through areas in buildings.

You begin the game with three lives. When you lose all three, the game is over. You may continue twice, giving you a cat-like nine lives in all. You can actually have unlimited continues by using passwords.

One of the items you start out with is a fist. While Eddie is not the world's greatest fighter, there are times he must defend himself or Roger. If you hold down button B for a couple of seconds, Eddie winds up and lets loose a much harder punch. You must be careful, however—when he's winding up, he's much more vulnerable to attack. Timing is everything.

Moving On

You begin the game in front of Eddie's office. Be sure to pick up the wallet lying on the ground, but be careful of falling objects. You can use the wallet to buy some of the items that you can't find for free. If you ever need money, you can come back to the office and search through the drawers to find another wallet. When you come out of the office, you'll find another wallet lying on the ground.

To beat this game, search through all of the buildings and the other areas of the city for clues and items. Be careful crossing the streets. Don't let Eddie get run over by a passing car! You don't have to worry so much about Roger with cars —he's a toon; if he gets run over, he'll just pop right back up. You do have to worry about the bird, however. Whenever you're outside, watch out—the bird can swoop down and snatch Roger, and you're out one more life.

If you take too long getting to the next place to search, the Weasels will come after Roger. To free him from the Wea sels you will have to answer silly riddles to make the Weasels laugh. If you're wrong, Roger gets it and you lose one of your lives.

Master Tips

❏ You will need the flashlight and the jumping shoes to explore the cave in the park. Watch out for the deadly snake that's guarding part of Acme's will.

❏ If you have the whistle, move Eddie into the road and blow the whistle to call Benny the Cab. Without the whistle, you'll have to find out where Benny is. When you find him, use the Select button to climb in. Use the arrow buttons to steer. A is the gas, and B is the brakes. Take off!

❏ Remember, Benny can't leave the road, but you need him to get through the tunnels leading to other parts of the town. Benny can also run over the Weasels to keep Roger from being captured. But remember—the Weasels are toons too! Hit 'em and they get right back up.

Pac-Man

Manufacturer: *Tengen*

Up Front

While all the players in your family will get a kick out of Pac-Man, it's included in the Titles for Tots section because it's so simple. This game is perfectly suited to young players who do not yet have the coordination necessary to manipulate some of the more complex games.

The Pac-Man concept is extremely basic. The screen is arranged in a maze-like structure. The paths that Pac-Man travels are littered with dots. To score points, you eat dots.

Pac-Man is pursued by four ghosts—Inky, Blinky, Pinky and Clyde. These ghosts want to eat Pac-man, but he can turn the tables on them by eating an energy pill which turns the ghosts blue and makes them vulnerable. Pac-Man can then eat the ghosts. Be careful though, they turn back to normal quickly, which means that Pac-Man again becomes the hunted rather than the hunter.

Competition is based on beating your own previous high score, or in taking on a second player and beating their score.

Despite the simple concept of this game, it'll take you a while to master it. The more mazes you go through, the faster it gets—the ghosts won't stay vulnerable for long.

Getting Started

The only controls you need are the four arrow buttons. They make Pac-Man travel up, down, left, and right. Once Pac-Man is traveling in the proper direction, you can let go of the key and he will continue in that direction until he comes to an obstacle. A joy-stick makes this game much easier for young children and makes it much closer to the way it was played on arcade machines.

Moving On

The best strategy to follow in playing the game is to clear out sections of dots as quickly as possible before eating the energy pill in that corner. Play cat and mouse with the ghosts, luring them into your corner, then eat the pill and go after them. When they begin to blink, the pill is wearing off—the ghosts could become deadly at any second.

Master Tips

❏ Even though this game is pretty simple, we can offer several tips to make you succeed. The first is to save the energy pills until you have cleared out a section.

❏ Secondly, don't leave a small section of dots in the maze; that makes it impossible for you to get Pac-Man back into that area later, and you may be unable to complete the maze.

❏ Lure as many of the ghosts into the area as possible before eating the pill. The first ghost Pac-Man gobbles is worth 200 points; after that, they double in value. Eating all four ghosts on one pill will get you 3000 points!

❏ As you move through the mazes, keep an eye under the center box (where the ghosts come from) for fruits. Pac-Man can eat these for extra bonus points, but it's kind of risky.

❏ Although it may not seem like it, the ghosts often pursue a preset path. Even though one may be on your tail, don't give up—it may unexpectedly veer off into another direction. If you have a good memory for mazes, you will begin to recognize patterns in the ghost's movements, allowing you to know in advance what paths are safe for Pac-Man to take.

Rampage

Manufacturer: *Data East*

Up Front

Take a scenic tour of America. Visit all the major cities and . . . trash them!

That's the idea behind Rampage, the game where you can be George the Ape or Lizzie the Lizard (similar to King Kong and Godzilla) and go on a rampage. Your mission, should you choose to accept it, is to flatten every major metropolitan area in the U.S. Great for kids and adults alike. While this game may not be everybody's cup of tea, it is an interesting twist to the usual "Save the World" plots.

Despite its violent content (as the monster, it is your job to trash buildings, eat people, crash helicopters, etc.), this game is suited to very young players because there are no really hard maneuvers. And, since there are unlimited continues available, even someone with zero coordination can get to the end of the game simply by being stubborn enough.

Getting Started

To begin the game, choose which monster, George or Lizzie, you want to be, then press the Start button.

If you begin the game in the one-player mode, another player can join you by pressing the B button on controller two.

The following controls will let you move your monster around the screen and perform the necessary acts of destruction:

↕	Go up and down the sides of buildings.
◀▶	Move left and right across the screen.
Ⓐ	Punch.
Ⓑ	Jump.

For additional destructive power, hold down button B. The monster pounces on objects that are lying on the ground.

Your main purpose in life is to punch holes in the sides of buildings until they come crashing down. But watch out for grenades, helicopter gunships, and tanks (among other enemies) while you're going about your business.

As you punch holes in the buildings, you will find a variety of objects, some of which are good to eat and will restore your strength. The nourishing goodies include milk, turkey, coffee, melons, fruits, toast, hamburgers and goldfish—in their bowls, of course! If you're still hungry, eat the people you come across for extra points.

Many times, you will see people jump out of the building and try to run. Chase them and eat them—you'll find that they give you a lot more strength than a turkey and goldfish sandwich.

Along the way, you will also find a variety of things that you shouldn't eat, including cactus plants, skulls, toasters, candles, lamps (if they're on), and toilets. These objects will sap your strength.

Your tour of destruction has been mapped out for you in advance. There are 128 cities for you to destroy; one city per day for 128 days. Every seven days (screens) there is a Search Bonus Round. In the bonus round, there's only one building on the screen. One of the rooms in the building contains a vitamin. If you find the vitamin and eat it before the building collapses, your monster will regain all of its strength.

Moving On

While you're busy laying the city flat, you'll be attacked by the Army, the Air Force, and the cops—even everyday citizens will try to get their shots in. Tanks will fire on you. Helicopters will buzz you. Soldiers will throw grenades and shoot at you. In other words, you don't have many friends.

Four different types of soldiers will try to stop you. Some have guns, some grenades, and some parachute out of the sky. Eating any of these guys makes for big bonus points.

The fourth type of soldier is a guy with a bomb, who's not too bright. He'll run up and put the bomb down in an attempt to blow you up. More often than not, however, he'll put the bomb down where it will blow up one of the buildings. Let him do some of your work—wait until he puts the bomb down before dining.

One last tip for this section. When you've inflicted enough damage to collapse a building, you will see smoke and dust rising up from the foundation. This is a good sign that it's time for you to get off the building. If you're on it when it goes down, you'll get hurt.

Master Tips

❏ If you see thunderstorms moving onto the screen, watch out—you could get hit by a lightning bolt that will knock you off a building.

❑ If you see a photographer, eat him fast. If he takes a flash picture, it could make you fall off the building.

❑ If you take a bad hit or fall, your monster will be stunned. During this time, you're easy prey for the tanks and helicopters. Keep an eye on the strength meter at the top of the screen; if it gets low, you'd better have a snack.

❑ When your strength meter falls to zero, you're done for. Your monster will fall to the sidewalk and change into a human being. If you want to continue the game, press button B before he walks off the edge of the screen. This turns him back into a monster. If he makes it off the screen, you still have five seconds to press the button and continue the game.

❑ If you are in the two-player mode, keep an eye on the other monster. If he gets killed and turns human, you can get a lot of your strength back by (you guessed it) eating him.

ARCADE TITLES

Many of the games in this section first appeared as coin-operated games in video arcades. They usually feature an interesting story line, a fairly decent challenge, and plenty of action!

Arcade
Titles

1943—The Battle of Midway

Manufacturer: *Capcom*

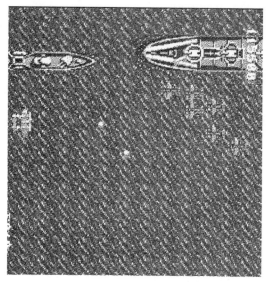

Up Front

With all due respect to our friends at Capcom, this game has about as much to do with the Battle of Midway as Iron Tank has to do with the Normandy Invasion. Nothing.

Instead of a lesson in history, we're treated to a rousing good shoot 'em up in a P-38 Mustang flier with some high-powered weapons that the current crop of fly boys would give their gold-framed portraits of Chuck Yeager to own.

You take on all comers, and there are plenty coming. Squadrons by air, flotillas by sea, anti-aircraft guns by land, all attempting to pommel you with bullets and missiles.

You only have one life to give for your country, but fortunately you have unlimited continues and a password feature to let you fight another day.

Getting Started

You view all of the action in this game from overhead, making the controls easy to master:

⬍◀▶	Control the P-38's position on the screen.
Ⓑ	Fire the weapons!
Ⓐ	Command energy-thirsty secret weapons (Lightning, Cyclone, and Tsunami) that make quick work of all enemies.
ⒶⒷ	Do a backover loop. (A good move for dodging some types of incoming fire.)

If your controller has turbo fire, you may want to turn it off. Holding down B powers up a laser weapon that can blast your opponents into oblivion. If you use turbo, the the laser shoots in quick pulses, never giving the laser time to charge up. When the weapon is fully charged, you'll hear a special charging sound—fire away.

Before you begin, the game displays five categories that can affect your plane's performance:

Offensive Power

Defensive Power

Energy Level

Special Weapons

Special Weapons Time Limit

Each category has six boxes beside it. The first box of each is filled in with red. You have three points that you can distribute anywhere you think will make your plane a better fighter. If you put points behind Offensive Power, your shots will have more effect on the enemy. If you put points behind Special Weapons Time limit, your power-ups will last longer. Plan your strategy.

At least once in each level you will uncover a point power-up. You will be taken immediately to this screen to put it where you want to add strength. You get through the level without being blasted in order to keep the point.

Moving On

 As you shoot down enemy planes and ships, other power-ups appear. 1943 has the most unique power-up system of any of the games included in this book. When the power-up first appears it is a POW (power) symbol. To turn it into another type of power-up (mostly special weapons), shoot it. The symbol cycles through all of the currently available power-ups and moves closer to the top of the screen. Since the screen slowly scrolls downward, this helps to keep the power-up in front of you where you can get at it. To collect the power-up, simply touch the nose of your plane to the symbol:

POW—energizes your plane.

Shot Gun—spreads the blast and neutralizes enemy fire.

3-Way Shot—shoots 3 different directions.

Auto—fires eight shots with a single press of button B.

Energy Tank—adds energy to the fighter. If you shoot a power-up too many times, it stays as an energy tank.

Super Shell—super effective shot.

Yashichi—this is the Japanese word for, "Restores max energy, dude."

Side Fighter—in later rounds you can have a twin at your side, as in Galaga.

In addition to the power-ups, you can get some really dumb bonuses. You'll see barrels, cows, spacemen, and other really out-of-place items. Touch them with the nose of the plane to earn energy or bonus points.

Master Tips

❑ There are two counters at the bottom of the screen: energy (E) and special weapon (SW). The SW counter shows how much time is left before your special weapon power-up runs out. The E shows you how much energy is left. Keep an eye on the meters.

❑ Unlike most games where energy equals life, you can still battle on when the energy meter hits 000. You won't be able to use the secret weapons, but you'll be alive. Just don't get hit! Getting hit is no big deal if you have lots of energy, but if you have none you're a goner.

❑ This is one fast and frantic game right from the start. Whole squadrons of planes come down on you. Until you get used to their patterns, try to keep the Shot Gun weapon. It is the only weapon capable of blasting enemy bullets.

❑ Some ships are longer than the screen is tall. Stay back and blast at the gun turrets as soon as they come on screen.

❑ Don't fool around so much with a power-up that you loose track of what's going on around you—you won't live to use it.

❑ Try to spray the whole screen with your guns to reveal hidden power-ups.

❑ Stay away from exploding enemies—the blast is deadly.

❑ If you have the energy and the enemies are closing in, remember to use the secret weapon to clear the screen.

Adventures of Dino Riki

Manufacturer: *Hudson Soft*

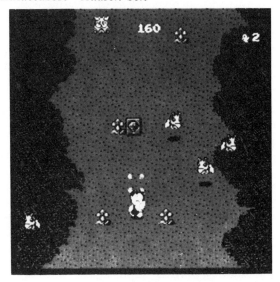

Up Front

It is the dawn of man. One particularly intelligent ancestor, Dino Riki, is out to "establish mankind's future in this violent age."

Forget the fact that, to the best of our scientific knowledge, people and dinosaurs were not on this Earth at the same time. Forget too that a world filled with monsters, quicksand, and a multitude of other hazards would not have been the best environment for human survival. And most important, don't forget to have fun with this Stone Age shoot 'em up.

The concept of this game is pretty simple. Shoot anything that gets in your way, dodge any incoming shots, and collect all the power-ups you can get your hands on. It looks easy, but this game presents a real challenge.

You have four weapons: rocks, axes, boomerangs, and torches. Each weapon is stronger than the one before. The problem is that each time you get hit, you lose your last weapon power-up. Unless you learn to dodge enemies and their fire, you won't get very far—you simply won't have the fire power.

There is a fifth fighting power-up, Macho Riki—your most powerful weapon of all. Since you can't use this weapon to fight the bosses at the end of each level, it isn't classified with the other weapons. When you collect the special Macho Riki power up, Dino is transformed into Macho, a mountain of muscle who shoots images of himself instead of fire or rocks.

To secure mankind's destiny, you must make it through four levels of dinosaurs, monster flies, skeletons that come to life, sinking lotus pads, and assorted prehistoric mutant monsters.

Getting Started

To begin the game, just press Start on the starting menu. During the game, use Start to pause the action and give Riki a breather. The other controls are fairly simple:

⬆⬅➡	Move Dino Riki around the screen.
Ⓐ	Fire weapons.
Ⓑ	Make Dino Riki jump. (When Dino has wings, hold down B to keep him flying.)

When the game begins, Dino Riki is in the desert. The screen begins scrolling upward. You can't stop it or slow it down. You will also see that no matter which way Dino Riki is facing, his shots always go up—to shoot your enemies, you must be below them.

In the upper left corner of the screen is a life meter made of hearts. When the hearts disappear, so does Mr. Riki.

Moving On

Blast all of the enemies and plants to reveal hidden power-ups. They are the secret to reaching the end:

Heart—adds a heart to the life meter.

Meat—restores the life meter.

Boots—increases Dino's speed.

Fist—upgrades weapon.

Bird—gives Riki the ability to fly one time.

Macho Riki—turns Dino into a super hero version of himself.

Diamond—get six of these without getting hit for a 1-up.

Star—destroys all enemies on screen.

When the action starts, you're in the desert. Blast everything you see—enemies *and* plants. By the time you get to the top of the screen, you'll have a much stronger weapon. You'll need this powerful weapon for what comes next.

Enemies come flying at you in waves. The trick to handling these enemies is to learn their patterns. Stand back and blast them as they come by in their neat little formations.

When you get to the lotus pad in the water, jump to it and use it as a bridge to get to level 1-1. Once you get past the puddles of water, stay to the right and shoot continuously to reveal hidden power-ups.

Watch out for the disappearing lotus pads in the water ahead. You can avoid some of the enemies by staying to the side and jumping along the water's edge. Jump to a lotus pad or start flying before the land runs out. If you fall in the water, you lose your life. Riki doesn't know how to swim!

When you get all the way to the top of the level, you'll see a door. The boss of level 1 is Pteranodon, a flying dinosaur. Stay at the bottom of the screen and blast away. It'll take several shots, but he goes down fairly easy.

In level 2 avoid the quicksand pits that open up under your feet. The enemies come at you hot and heavy. Keep an eye out especially for the fire breathing dinosaurs. Fly over their fire, or run past them between flares.

You will come to a blue wall that divides the screen into right and left paths. The path on the left has a Macho power-up. Get it.

The boss of level 2 is Tyrannosaurus. This guy's tough—it'll take several shots to bag him. If you have turbo fire, use it.

One of the flying enemies looks like a flock of black marbles. They circle you and begin closing in. Stand back from the top edge of their circle as far as you can and blast away at them. Our tester calls this "hosing them down."

In level three you'll meet some walking purple enemies. They don't die when you shoot them. Get past quickly or they'll get up and attack.

Master Tips

❏ When you get the Bird power-up, Dino sprouts wings. If you get a second Bird before you use the flying power-up, the wings will grow larger, giving you two flying power-ups.

❏ If you get hit in the air, you will fall to the ground. If you're over a hazard, you're a goner. If you have two flying power-ups, the first shot won't hurt you, but watch out for the second!

❏ One of the most effective fighting techniques for this game is to stay at the bottom of the screen and blast all of the enemies, then rush up and collect all of the power-ups before new enemies come at you.

❏ The boss in level three disappears and reappears. When he disappears, move down to the bottom of the screen and wait. If he reappears close to the bottom of the screen, move to the top to avoid his fire. Keep dodging till you can get a clean shot at him.

Back to the Future

Manufacturer: *LJN*

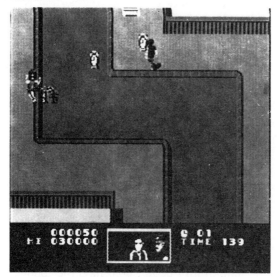

Up Front

Marty McFly has a problem. Marty jumped into the Professor's new Delorean sports car. But Marty doesn't know that the car is actually a time machine.

Suddenly he's transported back in time to his parents' high-school years. Worse yet, his mother has a crush on him. If he doesn't stop her, his slightly geeky father will never have a chance, and Marty won't be born! Marty must get things straight and get *Back to the Future*.

To do this he must skateboard past hordes of bullies, dodge flying food in the Cafe, play in the band, get his mother to kiss his father, and get the car back to the present. Just another day in Hill Valley.

Getting Started

You begin your journey through the town with four lives. At the bottom of the screen is your family portrait . . . it's fading before your very eyes.

To advance, you make your way through the streets and play arcade games. The street scenes are full of hazards and clocks. Each time you pick up a clock the portrait is restored for just a few seconds. The faster you pick up clocks, the better the picture looks. Another timer is also ticking away, counting down the time you have to make it through the block. To succeed, you must beat two clocks, the timer, and the clock that controls how quickly the picture fades.

The controls differ depending on which phase of the game you're in, but they're all fairly basic:

Street Game

⬍⬌	Move around the screen.
Ⓐ	Throw bowling balls.
Ⓐ	Jump.

Cafe Game

⬍⬌	Move from side to side behind the counter.
Ⓐ	Throw milk shakes.
Ⓑ	Activate the super shake.

School Game

⬍⬌	Move back and forth to block hearts.

Dance Hall Game

⬍⬌	Move with the other band members.

Driving Game

⬌	Steer the car.
⬍	Control the speed.

Moving On

When the game begins, you are walking to the Cafe, four blocks away. Each of the blocks is like a separate level. When you get to the end of the block, you find out how many bonus points you've earned.

You have 200 seconds to make it through each of the mazes (these seconds pass faster than real seconds.) Collect as many clocks as you can to keep the picture from fading away. When time runs out or the picture fades away, you lose your life and have to continue from the beginning of the level again. If you lose one of the arcade games, you must complete the last section of street again, then come back to the game.

As you walk along the street, you have to dodge bullies, bees, girls with hula hoops, benches, trash cans, and other assorted obstacles. Pass over every clock you can get to. They restore the picture a little. Each time you collect 100 clocks, you fully restore the picture.

Along the way you'll find a bowling ball. Throw the bowling ball with button B to knock down obstacles for bonus points. The ball won't hurt some of the obstacles—you'll have to jump over them instead or run around them.

When you see the skateboard, go for it. This doubles your speed. Run over clocks and run around anything else.

If you hit an obstacle, you'll fall flat on your face. It takes a few seconds to get back up. When you do, you won't have your bowling ball and skateboard. Don't worry—you'll get them back soon enough.

After you complete each block, you receive bonus points for every second left on the clock. You also get a 1-up for every 30,000 points.

In the next block, the Cafe Game, you'll find yourself behind a soda fountain counter. You move from side to side throwing milkshakes at the approaching bullies. You get 100 points for each bully you hit. Don't let even one bully get to the counter—he will slide you down the counter and into the doors at the top of the screen. Unless you've hit at least 50 bullies, you'll lose a life and have to go through the last street maze again.

A waitress on roller skates brings you super shakes. You begin with one super shake. When you have too many bullies on the screen to handle, press B to activate the super shake. This clears the screen and gives you one second to catch your breath.

Some of the bullies throw ice cream at you. If you get hit, it'll stun you for a second or two, letting the bullies attack the counter. Be careful!

Next, you must skate to the School Game. When you get there, you'll find yourself behind the teacher's desk in Science class. Yeech! Your mom is throwing heart shaped kisses at you. Use the book to block them. For every two hearts you block, you'll score one point on the game meter. You must score at least 50 to get by this game.

Next is the Dance Hall Game where you play in the band. The worst part is that you don't know any of the band members. Play some romantic music, so your father will kiss your mother. Only then can you advance.

Now that you've succeeded in getting your parents back together, you need to get back to the future. In the Driving Game you must steer the car around obstacles and lightning bolts at exactly the right speed (88) and touch the wire at the precise moment the lightning strikes it.

Master Tips

❏ With each level it gets harder to make it through the streets. When riding the skateboard, watch out for cracks and holes in the street. Many won't affect you when you're walking, but if you're on a skateboard and you don't jump at just the right time, you'll be lying face down on the pavement.

❏ When you have the bowling ball and the skateboard, you'll see bowling pins set up in the street. Bowl them over for 500 bonus points.

❏ There are rhythms to the arcade games that you can pick up on and use to your advantage. Try to get a feel for them.

❏ Those guys are carrying glass window panes. Don't try to go between them.

❏ You can't jump over benches.

Bad Dudes

Manufacturer: *Data East*

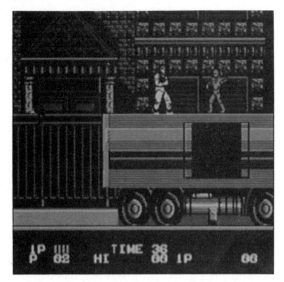

Up Front

The President is missing! Kidnapped by the Dragon Ninja. You will have to fight through city and forest, sewer and cave, on top of moving trucks and trains, and through the factory to get him back. Along the way you will have to fight the clock and hordes of ninjas, samurai, Super Warriors, and even a few fanatic girls.

Are you ready to prove that you are the baddest of the Bad Dudes? Will you live to hear the President say, "Hey, dudes, thanks for rescuing me. Let's go get a burger." Probably not, but it's worth a try.

Great music and fine graphics enhance this blast from the arcade as you take on level after level of fighting fun.

Getting Started

Select a one-player or two-player game with Select, then press Start to begin the game. Use the controls to make a variety of martial arts moves:

◀▶	Move side to side.
▲	Throw an uppercut.
▼	Duck a punch.
Ⓐ	Kick an enemy up close or punch one from a distance.
ⒶⒷ	When you're moving, this triggers a round-house kick that knocks out your opponent.
Ⓐ▼	Duck and punch, or pick up an item.
Ⓑ	Jump.
▲▼	Jump to a higher level when there is more than one path.
Ⓑ▼	Jump to a lower level.

As you fight your way to the President, you will gain certain items. Two of these are weapons: nun'chucks and knives, but you can have only one weapon at a time. If you like the weapon you have, don't pick up the other one. Soda cans will give you extra energy. The clock will give you extra time.

Some ninjas will throw spikes on the ground. Kick them out of the way or jump over them. DON'T step on them.

Moving On

When you encounter Super Warriors at the end of the levels, they have a life meter similar to yours but you will probably be too busy fighting them to look at it much.

If you get killed off, you won't have a weapon when you continue.

The boss at the end of the sewer scene transforms himself into five ninjas. Stay on the top level and beat them off two at a time, then get in a few whacks at the boss. While he's transforming you can't hurt him. Back off and take the little guys on first, then do as much damage as you can before he goes into his trance.

Stay on the high path in level four to avoid the dogs.

When you meet the robot ninja, get in a few quick punches, then stand back while he does his fancy kick—move in and blast him one in the chops.

Samurai try to sneak up on you and jump over your head. That's not so bad, but when they come down they hold swords aimed at your head. Don't let them jump. Punch them and they will jump to the side—then finish 'em off.

In the cave you must watch for falling stalactites. The thin blue ones are just about ready to fall—don't walk under them.

Master Tips

❏ If you hold down the button A until your character begins to flash, you can deliver a Super Punch that will take out the baddest enemy.

❏ Would you like to start with 63 lives? Try this:

On controller 2—press Ⓑ, Ⓐ, ⬇, ⬆, ⬇, ⬆.

On controller 1—press Start.

Double Dragon II

Manufacturer: *Tradewest*

Up Front

Nuclear war and its after-effects have devastated your little corner of the world. Thugs and hooligans going by the name of the Black Shadow Warriors invade the Double Dragon Dojo where the good guys work out. Although the Double Dragons put up a valiant struggle, they are overcome. In the melee the worst has happened. They gunned down your girlfriend.

You and your brother are all that is left of the Double Dragons, and you are bent on avenging sweet Marion in this arcade Armageddon.

There are a lot of ways to play this game. In addition to the one-player mode, you have two different two-player games. In the A version you and your brother cooperate. In the B version you can either cooperate or pound on each other. You're still trying to beat the bad guys, but you get to bop each other as well.

Once you have selected the number of players and the mode of play, you then have three different skill levels to choose from. The practice round gives you three levels of fairly easy stuff, so you can learn the moves and try out some different strategies. The Warrior level is just about the same as the arcade version of this game and has eight levels. The Supreme Master level is harder and contains an extra level where you fight the power behind the Black Shadow punks.

Getting Started

To master this game, you have to learn a few martial arts moves. Because this game began as an arcade hit, the control buttons work a little differently from most Nintendo adventures:

Ⓐ	Punch enemies on your right. (No need to turn before punching—this is real Ninja stuff.)
Ⓑ	Punch to your left.
ⒶⒷ	Jump.
Ⓐ	Facing right, punch to the right; facing left, kick to the left.
Ⓑ	Facing left, punch to the left; facing right, kicks to the right.

Ⓐ Ⓑ   Jump, then press the button in the direction
you want to kick. If you are moving when you
jump, and you have good timing, you throw a
Spinning Cyclone jump kick that is devastating.

To grab an enemy, punch them several times until their
head drops down slightly, then press the arrow in the direction
of that enemy. Once you got him, try these moves:

Noggin Knocker—Press button A or B several times
quickly in the enemy's direction.

Throw—Grab the enemy's hair and press the opposite
button to throw him over your shoulder.

Upper Kick—Press the up arrow and button A or B in
the direction you're facing.

Elbow Drop—Use the down arrow and the button for the
side you're facing.

There are two special moves that you can use to destroy
your enemy—the Hyper Uppercut and the High Knee Kick.
Both of these moves require you to be in a squatting position,
which is assumed when you land from a jump or are getting
up off the floor. You need to learn the precise timing for these
moves, but they're well worth learning.

To throw a Hyper Uppercut press the attack button of
your choice while in a squat. Use High Knee Kick by pressing
the arrow button in the direction of the enemy and pressing A
and B together.

Moving On

Your first mission is to invade the Shadow Warriors' home turf
in the inner city. When the play screen appears, you'll see a
status area at the bottom that shows your points earned, your
energy, remaining lives, and the high score of the day. There
is a separate display for each player.

Almost immediately, enemies start attacking. As you get
closer, more opponents begin to attack—and these guys are
tougher. As you clear the screens of attackers, a hand may
appear, pointing to the next place you must go. This is not a
trick of the Shadow Warrior—you can trust these directions.

One of your adversaries may carry a weapon. If you're
lucky enough to land a good punch, you might be able to dis-

arm them and use the weapon against them. You can't keep the weapon, however—you can only use it on the guy you took it from. As soon as you leave the screen (or sooner), the weapon is gone.

By the time you get to the boss, you better be getting a feel for some of the action moves, because the boss of the level is one tough cookie.

This boss goes running around wearing something that looks like a welder's mask. He might disappear, but don't relax, you haven't knocked him off. If you haven't learned how to use High Knee Kicks by now, you'd better learn fast!

The second mission takes you to the heliport where you'll have to empty out one helicopter and get on another. As you climb up the ladder, dodge the fire from the helicopter. Climb to the top and get those guys jumping out of the chopper in pairs. It won't take long to scare them off. Move to the right and start taking on the big chopper. The boss here is no big problem, just remember those High Knee Kicks.

In the third level you jump onto the big chopper just as it's taking off. As you fight off the bad guys, watch for the door to open. If you're near to it when it opens, you'll get sucked out. Stick with it, stay to the left as much as possible, and you'll make it.

Master Tips

- ❏ In level 5, watch out for mini-bosses coming out of the cabin. To get them in one shot, High Knee them off the cliff.
- ❏ In level 6 watch out for falling fire and disappearing steps.
- ❏ To get past the moving gears, wait till they stop—jump on them and then over. If they start spinning while you're on one, jump for your life!
- ❏ Even though a boss is invisible, you can still hurt him, you just need to know where he is.
- ❏ In the two-player B game you can take lives away from your brother by knocking him off. Play alone and choose the B variation. You have to protect your brother while you knock off the bad guys, but when you're alone with

him you can beat up on him for extra points. Each time you knock him off, you get an extra life. What are brothers for, anyway?

Marble Madness

Manufacturer: *Milton Bradley*

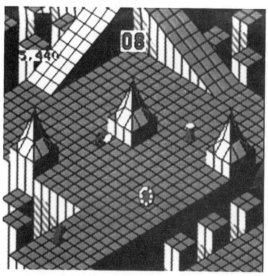

Up Front

In this game the purpose is to run your marble through an increasingly difficult set of mazes. You encounter killer marbles, marble munchers, and pools of acid, not to mention the hammers and spikes. Except for the screams of marbles falling to their deaths as they plunge over the cliffs, this game is violence free.

While this game is easy enough for a five-year-old to enjoy, it's challenging enough so that parents will love to play long after the kiddies are in bed. These mazes are a real challenge.

Getting Started

A joystick comes in handy in Marble Madness—trying to make the necessary moves with a controller pad is a bit on the tricky side.

The game offers two choices for using the controller. You can choose to hold the controller at a 90-degree angle (the normal controller position for most other games) or tilt the controller at a 45-degree angle. Most players find the 45-degree setting a little easier to handle.

After you enter your name, the game starts you off in the practice round. Here you pass through a very simple maze just to get the hang of things. It also gives you a chance to earn points and bonus time.

In Marble Madness you play against the clock. You have a set number of seconds to move the marble through the maze. If you lose the marble over the edge of a cliff, you get another marble. Unfortunately you don't get another marble instantly—you're penalized a couple of seconds for messing up.

If you reach the goal line with time to spare, you earn bonus points and extra time to complete the next maze. This extra time really helps later—the mazes get harder and harder.

When you fail to complete a maze in the allotted time, the game ends and you must start over from the practice round. You even have to enter your name again. Oh well, kids love repetition—just ask any parent who has had to put up with six showings of *Batman* in the same weekend!

Moving On

Every once in awhile a magic wand appears and gives you ten extra seconds to finish the maze. Usually this is great, but the wand may pop up at a time when you're delicately maneuvering the marble near a ledge. The screen freezes, and as soon as the magic wand disappears, so does the marble—right into a bottomless pit.

So now you only have eight of the extra ten seconds given to you by the wand. Whatever happens, don't squander this time! Keep moving through the maze and get to the goal as quickly as possible so you'll get those extra points and bonus time.

The two-player mode is more fun than should legally be allowed, as you battle the other player to make it through the maze first. If you want to be mean, you can bash into your opponent's marble and send them, Ahhh!, over the edge.

A more effective strategy, although it may not be as much fun, is simply to outrace your opponent. This really messes up their movements. The screen follows the leader's marble. As you move down in the maze the other marble disappears and rematerializes (at a cost of lost seconds) further down.

If your competition is on a ledge and has a button pushed down when the marble rematerializes, they start moving in that direction. About half the time this sends them twirling over the edge. It'll drive your opponent crazy!

Remember, if you fall behind, the game will move you ahead in the maze, but it'll penalize you. You may cross the finish line first, but you'll lose time and bonus points.

Master Tips

❏ When you get bumped by Marble Munchers, bump into walls, or drop off a ledge onto a hard surface, your marble gets stars and spinnies much like Roger Rabbit after the refrigerator drops on his head. When you can see the stars on screen, your marble is sluggish. If you're in a delicate place in the maze, slow down and let the marble recover.

❏ You can earn extra points by finding shortcuts, beating the black marble, or taking more difficult paths. While these extra points may take you a touch further up the top ten scorers chart, they won't always help you get to the end of the mazes quicker.

❏ One way to get the most time for each of the mazes is to play in the two-player mode and just ignore the second controller. That way you win the bonus time for *beating* the other guy. Kind of a cheap way of earning points, but it works.

❏ Level five is the silly race. Everything is topsy-turvy. If you mess up, you lose precious time. Mash the little vermin that get in your way to earn as much time as you can—it takes at least fifty seconds to complete the last maze successfully.

❏ The key to mastering Marble Madness is repetition. You must learn the early mazes by heart in order to get to the next levels with enough time remaining to win.

RoadBlasters

Manufacturer: *Mindscape*

Up Front

Head out onto the open road and mow down everything in your path! That's the idea behind this arcade style shoot em' up on wheels. There is no plot, no princess to save, no evil bosses to beat, no saving the world, just fifty levels of high-speed bumper car fun.

Each of the fifty levels is organized as a rally. To get to the finish line you must keep your super-car fueled up by driving through green and orange fuel globes. All kinds of enemies will get in your way, shoot at you, drop land mines, and try to run you off the road.

You begin the game with three lives. Each time you run out of fuel, you lose a life. You can crash, get blasted, whatever, it doesn't matter. As long as you still have fuel, your car will reappear. Run out of fuel three times and the race is over, pal.

Getting Started

To begin the game, press any button. The level selection screen appears. Once you're there you can choose to start the game at level 1, 4, or 11. Use the arrow buttons to select your starting point, then press Start. Use the following controls to maneuver your car:

←	Accelerate to a top speed of 212 miles per hour. (When you're at the speed you want, you don't have to hold down the button.)
↓	Put on the brakes.
↔	Steer.
Ⓐ	Fire your guns!
Ⓑ	Activate special weapons.

As you race down the road you'll meet all sorts of half-crazed drivers. Blow them off the road before they can get a shot at you.

The most plentiful of these enemies are the orange cars called Stingers. In higher levels, these guys are the way you will get fuel. Some of them will turn into orange fuel globes when you blast them. These globes will travel down the road at cruising speed. Hurry!

Moving On

 Every so often the support jet comes down and drops power-ups for you to use. Position your car under the descending item or you'll miss it. Four different power-ups are available:

U.Z. Cannon—a roof-mounted rapid-fire gun with a longer range than the normal guns.

Nitro Inject—increases your top speed to 298 miles per hour for a short burst of speed. You can use it only three times.

Electro Shield—makes you invulnerable for short periods of time. You can use it only three times.

Cruise Missiles—clears the road ahead of you with one shot. Unfortunately it will also clear the road of fuel globes—be careful.

You begin each level with a full tank of fuel. Accelerate and get to cruising speed as quickly as you can. There's an automatic refuel about halfway through each level, but you will want to get as many fuel globes as possible.

The blue cars are command vehicles. You need to fire a Cruise Missile or the Electro Shield to destroy them.

Master Tips

❏ If a light on your dashboard starts blinking, you're getting close to land mines. You may want to slow down, unless you have the reflexes of a cat.

❏ Watch out for the radioactive oil slicks. If you hit one, you'll spin. If you're not close to any enemies, you may be alright. Otherwise, you'll spin right into the back of another car.

❏ In later levels you'll see green fuel globes on the side of the road. Since you need to pull off the road to get a refill, these slow you way down. Watch for enemies behind you.

❏ The orange things on the side of the road aren't fuel, they're rocks. Don't smack one trying to get gas.

❏ The rat jeeps come in from the side of the road and pull right in front of you. Then they slow way down. Whenever our tester blasts one of these dusty demons, she yells, "Take that you dirty grit!"

❏ You can bypass sections of the game. The game displays a selection screen like the one that starts the game. You have the choice to continue or to advance to one of three different levels. If you're doing well, take the step up. If you are just barely getting to the finish line, stay on the lower levels.

RoboCop

Manufacturer: *Data East*

Up Front

Things are bad in Detroit. The Tigers haven't won a pennant in years, the Lions haven't ever won a Super Bowl, the Japanese are selling cars like crazy, and crime is rampant in the streets. The police can't handle the situation. OPC corporation is seeking a contract to put the entire police force out of work by using RoboCops. Half man, half machine, totally mean!

There is of course no way to bring the complexity of the movie plot to a Nintendo game, but the violent overtones of the film have been well preserved in this futuristic shoot 'em up. As RoboCop it is your duty to go get the bad guys through six levels of non-stop action.

This is not the most challenging game in the action/ adventure category. The levels are fairly short and require very little in the way of investigation. But it's ideal for younger players.

Getting Started

Getting this game going is simple—just press Start. The controls are no great challenge either:

◀▶	Move RoboCop left and right.
▲	Aim upward and walk up stairs.
▼	Duck, pick up objects, and walk down stairs.
Select ▼	Block punches.
Ⓐ	Fire away!
Ⓑ	Throw a punch.

As RoboCop you must be conscious of both time and power represented by meters in the upper left of the screen. Run out of either and you're history.

When you're under heavy attack, press Select to become invulnerable temporarily—you'll lose a lot of energy, but it may be worth it.

As you move through the levels, you will find small bags of power (marked with a P) and batteries. Batteries will give you extra time to complete the level.

You have your choice of three different weapons. First is the Auto-9, RoboCop's special issue hand gun. In later levels you'll find a machine gun, which holds up to 50 shots, and the Cobra Gun.

To switch weapons press Start (pausing the game) and use the up arrow to cycle through the weapons you have. As each weapon appears in the box at the bottom of the screen, you can see how many bullets are left.

Four other indicators also appear on the screen. The face shield is the infrared vision indicator. When this blinks, look on the screen for a flashing area, then punch it. The fist symbol blinks when you need to punch out an enemy—that's the only way you can defeat him. The circular symbol is the foe indicator—when you're almost at the end of the level and you're near the enemy, this indicator starts blinking. The energy/power alarm sounds when you are draining energy at a great rate, or when your energy is dangerously low.

Moving On

The first level of RoboCop is easy—it's just an introduction to the game. Keep working to the right. At the end of the street is a warehouse where you will do battle with the first boss. Punch him out—your gun is ineffective.

In the second level you meet some wonderfully friendly guys with flamethrowers on your way to City Hall. Fortunately you can duck under their fire. When you get the chance, blast them out of the window.

When you get into City Hall be sure to check either the first or second door. The first door on the second floor is a shortcut to finding the mayor; he's being held hostage at gunpoint. When the mayor ducks, fire at the bad guy. If you hit the mayor, you lose energy. Besides, shooting the mayor is no way to get the key to the city.

In level three you raid the narcotics factory. Here you will find the Cobra Gun. You will also find a new piece of slime, Grenade Boy. To defeat this guy move in close and punch his lights out. Luckily when you get near the freight elevator, enemies disappear. If you're getting attacked, take advantage of this.

When you take the second elevator down to where the boss is, Grenade Boy shows up again. Jump back on the elevator and make your entrance again—you won't see Grenade Boy. You'll meet six bosses in level three. When you first walk into the room, blast the three guys there. Once they're out of the picture, quickly run to the right side of the room. Three more guys will jump off the top deck to get you. Crouch down and keep blasting.

Master Tips

❏ When you pick up a weapon that you already have, all of the ammunition for that weapon is replenished.

❏ If you get killed, all the weapons you have collected are taken away. It is nearly impossible to get through the sixth level without the Cobra Gun.

❏ Level six starts with a conveyer belt scene. Blast the helicopter out of the sky as soon as you can. Stay away from the left side of the screen. If you get too far to that side, the chopper will come back.

❏ There are unlimited continues if you know a secret. Hold down A, B, and Select, then press Start. But this still won't get you the Cobra Gun on level six!

Paperboy

Manufacturer: *Mindscape*

Up Front

You wake up just before sunrise. You wait at the corner with the guys, watching your breath in the chilly morning air. The truck comes around the corner and drops off the bundles of newspapers you've been waiting for. Quickly, expertly, you fold the papers into rock hard missiles. The better you fold 'em, the more accurately you can toss 'em. You never know when you might need to use them as weapons. Then you're off to deliver the news to all the houses on your route.

Paperboy's game play is a riot. Our tester demonstrated this game in the conference room of an insurance agency. In very little time he had an audience of adults cheering him on as he tossed papers through windows, at barking dogs, and through hedges. The groan of the crowd as the poor tyke got mowed down by a crazed motorcyclist was enough to break your heart.

Getting Started

The object of this game is to make each day's deliveries, get through the practice area, and cross the finish line. You make the required moves with the following controls:

⬍◀▶	Steer the bicycle.
Ⓐ or Ⓑ	Let that paper fly!

You begin with four lives and ten papers.

Moving On

Along the way, you'll come across bundles of papers in odd places along the route. Be sure to restock your paper supply from the bundle. This is the only object that you can run over without falling off your bike. If you fall off the bike, you lose a life. Kind of drastic, but, hey, you're going pretty fast.

Subscribers houses are white. Non-subscribers houses are red. Both types of houses have all kinds of stuff that gets in your way. Just don't hit any of it! Get a paper to each of your subscribers. Put a paper through the window of as many non-subscribers as you can.

Extra point bonuses are available by knocking things over and breaking them. If you get attacked by a running dog or a rolling tire, hit it with a paper to escape.

Master Tips

❏ Once you have completed your route, you can earn extra bonus points for making it through the paperboy's obstacle course. Jump ramps, avoid fences, and hit targets with papers all the way to the finish line to keep your subscribers.

❏ Remember that the up and down arrows control speed. You may have to outrun obstacles, but sometimes it's better to slow down and let them pass. Don't get carried away with speed.

❏ The automatic lawn mower usually won't get in your way unless you go into its territory.

Life Force

Manufacturer: *Konami*

Up Front

Life Force is a lot like Contra, except that the story does not take place on Earth, which is fortunate for us earthlings. You see, in Life Force, you must battle Zelos and his henchmen. It's not that Zelos is such a bad guy, it's just that he's hungry, very hungry. And when Zelos decides to eat out, he doesn't go down to the corner hot-dog stand—he chomps down whole planets. Fighting this guy is a bit like fighting your way through space and through his intestinal tract all at the same time.

Getting Started

To begin the game, choose to play with one or two players and press Start. Use the following controls to move around the screen and fire weapons:

☰◆◆   Move the fighter around and through the obstacles that Zelos throws in your path.

Ⓑ   Fire the various weapons.

   Power-ups are disguised as star-like shields with a red circle in them. These provide you with a variety of weapons that include laser fire, scatter fire, missiles, and even a companion phantom that fires along with you as it circles your ship. Fire high and it fires low. Swoop down and it takes up position on your topside and fires high.

Don't get knocked out of the sky. Every time you get blown up, you lose all of your power-ups and have to begin building your weapons again.

Moving On

The first level of the game is called Cell Stage 1. In this stage, you invade the body of Zelos. Watch out for chomping teeth, growing cell structures and opposing fighters. Waving arm-like structures reach out for you—dodge them!

You can't pass through anything that completely blocks the way. Sometimes, cell structures grow in front of your eyes. If you have a rapid fire or continuous fire option on your joystick, turn it on. You'll make better speed cutting through the tissues of the bloated beast.

At the end of the first stage, you come to a solid wall of tissue. It begins to glow. This is your first major challenge. You must defeat Golem to advance any further. Golem is an ugly beast with the same arm-like structures you've already seen. To defeat him, you must fire repeatedly into his eye.

Here's the trick—when he reaches for you with his arms, he starts moving toward the left. If you want to keep shooting into his eye, you need to keep him steady. Circle him, and let him reach to the right for you. As he does this, he moves to the right. Circle again and go for the eye.

The second level is called the Volcanic Stage. In this battle, you start flying straight up instead of left to right. Along the way, you encounter hordes of fighters and volcanic rock. You also come across indestructible meteors. Since blasting them won't do any good, dart past them as best you can.

Finally, you emerge into a big blue mechanical room guarded by three eyes—these are the guys you're after. Watch out for indestructible enemy eyeballs that come flying at you. Dodge these eyeballs and work your way under the three eyes you're after. Blast away each eye's protective plating, and the eyes become vulnerable—destroy them!

Once past this mess, you come nose to nose with Intruder, a mean machine with swinging arms of balls that can crush your ship. Only his eye is vulnerable to your fire. Circle clockwise with the arms and wait until the eye opens. When it opens, blast away. If you're fast enough, you can dodge the arms and blast the eye at close range to destroy it quickly.

In the Prominence Stage, you battle walls of flame that resemble the Banzai Pipeline. Fortunately, you get a warning before the flares erupt. Just before they erupt, a bump forms on the wall of flame. About a second later, the flare erupts, curling back over itself. If you can't get out of its path, back up and ride it out in the tube, surfer style.

The fourth level is called Cell Stage 2. In this level, you infiltrate the blood stream of the Bloated One. His immune system attacks you, fighters pounce on you, and all sorts of debris comes flying at your head—after all, this guy does eat planets for appetizers.

Eventually, you emerge into the ribcage of Zelos. Stay low to avoid the laser fire, and get ready to say hello to Giga. Giga is a skull-like boss who fires cells out of his mouth while his eyeballs circle for you. Watch his mouth; when it opens, fire away! Patience is the key for bagging this guy.

The final assault is called the Mechanical City Stage. This stage is fast and furious. You're climbing straight up to the center of Zelos—to attack his heart and soul!

 Hordes of fighters come at you. The red ones are well protected in their formations, but they're good for power-ups. As you come into the city, expect cannon fire from all sides. Be sure to take out the missiles on the sides of the walls—it's tough to outrun their fire. The stone heads spit hot rings of fire (cinnamon Life Savers?) at you. Try to blast as many as you can—they'll try to float up after you. Shoot at their mouths to take 'em out.

Fight your way through this, and you come upon Zelos' vitals, guarded by the grandest Tetron of them all. The Tetron weaves in and out of range. Aim for his head. Once you defeat him, an unknown force pulls you up. Blast the circular structure on Zelos' heart to blow it up.

All you have to do now is escape from Zelos' body before it explodes. You must make your way through a speed section so narrow and unforgiving that you may get your medals after you die.

If you have any fighters left over, you can start the mission again, except that this time it's not so easy.

Master Tips

- ❏ Want 30 fighters? Press Up, Up, Down, Down, Left, Right, Left, Right, B, A, and Start. Combined with three continues and 1-ups scattered around in the levels, this should be enough to get you there.

- ❏ If you get blasted, and you will, you'll be invulnerable for a brief period of time as your fighter recovers. Use this time to position yourself so that you won't get wasted again immediately. You can even fly through obstacles that would normally make you crash.

Action/Adventure games usually involve an interesting story and set you out on some sort of mission. You usually have to travel great distances, fight evil monsters, and save a world or two. The nice thing is you can usually finish the job in time for dinner!

Action/Adventure Titles

A Boy and His Blob

Manufacturer: *Absolute*

Up Front

A Boy and His Blob is one of the sweetest and most imaginative games to come along in a while. The hero of the story is the Boy—you'll have to give him a name. He is recruited by a friendly alien Blob named Blobert who's trying to save Blobolonia, his home planet.

The problem is that Blobs live on a steady diet of candy, jellybeans preferably, but the Evil Blob Emperor has taken all of the jellybeans for himself and forced the population of Blobolonia to live on nothing but chocolate kisses and marshmallows. While many Nintendo players would give their eye-teeth for such a diet (and some of them do), the Blobs don't like it a bit.

You, the boy, must first take on the hazards of a hidden world under the subway, where mysterious, indestructible Subway Serpents and rock showers guard a store of treasures.

Usually these treasures include tools you can use to fight your way through the maze. You take the tools with you in the form of a Blob. Blobert, you see, is a shape shifter. Different flavored jellybeans turn him into different objects, such as ladders, trampolines, umbrellas, and blowtorches. You'll soon catch onto the fact that there's a logical connection between the type of jellybean and what it does. For example, cinnamon jellybeans are hot—they turn Blobert into a blowtorch.

Gather enough treasures and you can take them to the Health Food Store for a supply of vitamins. These are the bane of the Evil Blob Emperor—they can kill him. This is the only violence in the game—if you can call pumping evil rulers full of vitamins violence.

Among the treasures hidden in the subway is a VitaBlaster, which uses vitamins as ammunition. With the VitaBlaster and a little courage you can triumph over the Evil Emperor. The Blobs, at long last, will be able to sit down to a decent meal.

Younger players will get a kick out of this game, while older players will find it a taxing mental challenge as well. This game's a real mind bender!

Getting Started

When the game starts, the boy and the Blob are standing on the sidewalk in front of the boy's house. At the top of the screen is a status line that shows how many points you've earned, how many treasures are left to find, and how many lives you have. You begin with five lives. Get killed too many times and the game is over. There's no continue feature in this game. Use the following controls to move the boy:

⬌⬍	Move the boy along the street. As the boy moves, Blobert follows.
Ⓑ	If Blobert isn't quick enough, press button B to whistle for him. You can also whistle to move him into a different position.
Ⓐ	Feed Blobert a jellybean. Make sure you're facing him and that you've selected the flavor you want with the Select button.

If you are too close or too far away, the jelly bean will miss Blobert's mouth—he'll pout until you feed him a jellybean. Remember, each different flavor will turn Blobert into a different shape or tool. To return him to his normal state, just whistle.

When you get into the subway, look around. You will find the first treasure immediately. Now all you have to do is to experiment to find out how to get there!

Moving On

One thing you need to know is that the boy can jump down a short distance without getting hurt. If he falls much farther than one and a half screens, though, he's history.

If you come to a place where there's an obvious drop-off, toss a jellybean over the side to see what is down there. You can throw the jellybean farther by stepping forward as you throw.

To find more treasures, you have to get into the caverns under the subway. Here's the one and only hint you need. Punch flavored jellybeans *punch* holes in whatever you're standing on. Move along the platform to where the graffiti is painted on the wall. Punch a hole in the floor just under the "-by" in Baby and step down. Here you will find your second treasure, but be careful!

The second treasure is guarded by one of the indestructible Subway Serpents. You can't hurt this guy. The only chance you have is to run under him when he's at the highest point in his jump. Timing is everything!

In the underground caverns you find all sorts of treasures—bags of jellybeans and chests of jewels and diamonds. Two of these are tough to get.

At the bottom of the ocean is a chest of jewels. Be careful, it's guarded by sharp pointed rocks that can burst your bubble. By the way, the boy can't swim.

You can find another chest of jewels on a rocky ledge, guarded by a serpent. You have to time your jump down onto the ledge, turn Blobert into a ladder, get the jewels, and get back up while dodging the serpent as it jumps back and forth over your head. It's not as easy as it sounds! The other method is to punch down through the floor, but then you'll have a long way to go to get back on track.

You can skip these two treasures and still amass enough vitamins to win the game. But if you can get these treasures, you can really impress your friends. Getting the underwater treasure chest is the hardest thing to do in the entire game!

One of the last treasures you'll find is a bag of jellybeans that includes two new flavors. One of these activates the VitaBlaster. Once out of the subway, make your way to the Health Food Store to get your vitamins—ammunition for the VitaBlaster.

Master Tips

❏ The second stage of the game takes place on the planet of Blobolonia, the home of the Blobs. Use your special type of transportation to get there.

❏ On Blobolonia collect all the peppermints you can find. For every five, you get a life. Some are hidden in underground caverns, while some hang in the air just out of view. Turn Blobert into a trampoline to jump up and find them.

❏ If you have trouble getting Blobert into the right position to turn him into a trampoline, turn him into a blowtorch or some other object that you can pick up. Get him in the right position, then press A to set him down.

❏ The hardest part of the second stage is getting through the first set of screens. You have to dodge bouncing marshmallows and deal with cherry bombs. There's no way to kill the marshmallows—step between them as they bounce up over your head. Watch the background to find the spots between the marshmallows. Move in before the marshmallow comes bouncing down again. It takes patience, patience, and more patience.

❏ Once you've made it past the marshmallows, move to the next screen. If you back up into the screen you just came from, the marshmallows are gone and you can hunt for peppermints.

❏ After you get past the last screenful of marshmallows, watch out—the next several screens are loaded with cherry bombs. If even one cherry bomb touches the ground, you're dead. You can't run back to the previous screen for safety either—the bombs will still kill you. As you clear each screen of its obstacles, look for peppermints.

❏ Remember, there's no continue feature. If you get killed off, you have to go back to the subway and collect the treasures all over again!

❏ The final part of the battle involves getting past the killer popcorn, making it through the candy factory, and passing through the caves to the emperor's lair. Once you're past the popcorn, the rest is a cake walk! You need to use your head more than anything else.

❏ Once you are inside the cave of the emperor, you'll come to a spot where chocolate kisses and peppermints come drifting up from below. Use the VitaBlaster to knock off the chocolate kisses without killing off the peppermints. After you've killed the kisses, put a bridge over the gorge and stand in the middle absorbing peppermints. The mints keep coming until you have as many as nine lives. Meow! Get as many lives as you can—the last big obstacle is yet to come.

❏ The passageway leading to the emperor is lined with big chomping teeth! Use the same technique for getting through the teeth as you did to get through the bouncing marshmallows. Watch for patterns!

❏ The very end of the game begins with the emperor kidnapping and caging poor Blobert! Think! How the evil one gets it in the end is a real surprise!

Astyanax

Manufacturer: *Jaleco*

Up Front

Ok, so maybe its a little weird that your parents named you Astyanax (As-tie-in-knacks), but hey, some parents are still a little wigged out from the Sixties. What's really strange is this dream you've been having about a girl trapped in a bubble. Maybe it's the lack of sleep from all that late night studying for Algebra class.

As you head home from school one afternoon, everything starts to look strange. The sky changes colors and the sun becomes a purple ball of fire. Hey! Where did you go?

You're at the Gate of Remila. Hovering around you is a fairy named Cutie who explains to you that the girl in the bubble is the Princess Rosebud, held captive by the Evil Blackthorn. Blackthorn plans to drain her magic powers and rule the world. Only you can stop him. You'd better not fail, for only Princess Rosebud can return you to your own world.

The story unfolds as in a movie. Great graphics and music make it a pleasure to play. Although you don't get to fight a lot of different enemy monsters, the action is as tough as it comes. It took our tester a week to win this game instead of his usual day and a half. According to him this is one of the hardest games he's ever played.

Getting Started

Astyanax has no passwords. Keep going or start over. There are unlimited continues, but you don't want to go into the last level without the sword (Astyanax's most powerful weapon).

The Start button begins the game. During the game, press Start to pause the action and to bypass the movie-like parts of the game.

Use Start and the up arrow to choose one of three magic spells. Bind stops time and uses the least energy. Blast wounds all enemies on screen and uses less energy than Bolt. Bolt is the most powerful spell, making minced meat out of all the enemies on screen, but it uses a lot of energy. You can also use Start to continue from the last level when you lose all your lives. Use the following controls to move Astyanax:

◀▶	Move Astyanax left and right.
▼	Duck under danger.
▲ Ⓑ	Cast a magic spell.
Ⓐ	Jump.

At the bottom of the screen is a status board. It shows how many lives remain, the score (1-ups are awarded for high scores), the selected spell, and the level you are on. In addition, you see three meters. The PW (power of weapon) meter shows how powerful the next hit will be. This meter changes a lot as you play. The LF (Life Force) meter shows how much damage Astyanax can take. When all the hearts are gone, so is he. The last meter, SP (Spell Power), shows how much magic is left. If you've used up all of the magic, Cutie may recharge you, but then again she may not.

You begin each level with a full charge of life and spell power.

When you begin the game, Cutie gives you an ax. Chop at the stone statues to find different power-ups. Among these power-ups is an ax symbol that gives you a different weapon. The ax changes to the spear and the spear changes to the sword. The ax is medium, the spear does the least harm and takes the least spell energy, and the sword (because it is the most powerful) can do the most harm and takes the most power.

Other power-ups include potions to refresh life, extra weapon power, 1-ups, wings to swing weapons faster, and Cutie, herself. When you find Cutie, you will get your choice of a new weapon or a Spell Power power-up.

Each time you get killed off, you continue with the next lower weapon. The sword becomes a spear, and the spear becomes the ax.

Moving On

To win the game, you must clear six challenging levels. Although you won't meet very many different monsters, each one you meet has a special strength. Different colors represent different strengths.

As you hack your way through Level 1-1, save your magic for Ceasar, the mini-boss. You'll meet this guy at the end. Blast him with Bolt magic, then attack him quickly before he has a chance to use his magic on you.

To beat the Medusa at the end of 2-2, crouch down and hit at the crystal around her neck. When the snakes jump at you from the head of Medusa, be close enough so that they go over your head. Medusa won't come any closer. Whack the snakes, then go back to the crystal. When Medusa disappears, be ready for her on the other side of the screen and repeat the action.

At the end of 3-2 you meet a particularly nasty varmint. He first appears as a rock. Use magic and your sword (by now you should have it) to smash his mask. Start working on his face until the rock explodes. Now, you have to deal with a little red creature that floats around and spits poison bubbles at you. Get in as many licks as you can before he speeds up.

Level 4-1 starts out the Marshy sequence. There are two new enemies here: little flying fish and big flying fish. The little ones may annoy you, but they don't do much else. The big green flying fish come up out of the water and try to poke you with spears. Keep your distance and keep hacking.

Save lots of spell power for the end of 4-2—you'll have two bosses to defeat.

Master Tips

❏ In the castle, you'll see many doors. Go through the ones defended by the golden skeletons. If you go through any of the other doors, you'll be sent back to a place you've already been.

❏ To defeat Thorndog, chop his hand off and whack the crystal around his neck. When his hand grows back, crouch down and stay between him and the bolt of electricity he shoots through his fingers. When his blast is over, chop off his hand again and go back to work on the crystal.

❏ In the last level you meet the major bosses again—use your magic wisely.

❏ Save your magic as much as possible while playing through the levels, but if you have too many enemies attacking you, use Bolt magic to clear the screen.

Batman

Manufacturer: *Sunsoft*

Up Front

Gotham City is trying to celebrate its two-hundred year anniversary. But the Joker and his gruesome gang have plans of their own. Only one person can save the city and get rid of the Joker's slimy crew—Batman.

As Batman you must fight your way through five levels of nasties in order to get to the final showdown . . . with the Joker himself! You have four weapons:

Your fists	You can defeat most enemies simply by punching them. All of the other weapons have limited ammunition. Use your fists, and save the others for bigger fights.
Spear Gun	This weapon shoots short spears.
Batarang	Batman's deadly version of the boomerang. Sometimes one shot will count as two because the Batarang will hit the enemy again as it comes back to Batman.
Dirk	The most powerful of Batman's weapons, Dirk fires three shots at the same time.

Getting Started

To begin the game, press Start. Then use the following controls to move Batman and fight the criminals:

◀▶	Move Batman around the screen.
▼	Crouch to duck punches.
Ⓐ	Jump up.
Ⓑ	Punch or fire your weapons if you have ammunition power-ups.
Start	Change from one weapon to another.
Select	Pause the action and display your score.

The instruction booklet doesn't mention much about Batman's climbing ability, but if you want to get through the early stages, you'd better learn how to climb. If you've ever played Ninja Gaiden, you already know how to do it. If you jump onto a wall, Batman grabs hold of it for just a second (unlike Ninja Gaiden, you can't stay there as long as you want). If you jump while clinging to the wall, you move up in the opposite direction. Batman zig-zags up the walls.

 Only a few Bat-items (power-ups) are available. You earn them by defeating enemies:

Blue blocks marked with a B—bonus points.
Blue blocks with a rocket—power up Batman's weapons. Each weapon uses a different amount of energy. The highest the counter goes is 99. Use it or loose it.
Hearts—restore one block of Batman's life meter. Guess what happens when the meter gets to zero. Go on, guess.

There are no passwords, but you may continue as many times as you like.

Moving On

Level 1 begins in a deserted shopping mall. Move to your right and watch out for the roving land mines. To get rid of these pests, crouch down and punch them.

You'd better get used to the flamethrower guy—you'll see him a lot. His flamethrower has limited range. Stay back until he's fired his burst of shots, then move in quick and punch him out.

When you get to the corner—you'll see the DON'T WALK sign—you're about to encounter Deadshot and his brothers for the first time. Duck under the shot from his gun, then punch him out too.

By this time you should have plenty of power for your weapons. Feel free to use one of them if you think you need to, even if we say punch. It's your choice.

To choose your weapon, press Start to cycle through them. A picture of the weapon appears above your life meter. When you are done with your weapon, cycle back so that the area above the meter says Batman. Getting into the habit of doing this will keep you from wasting ammo.

Next, you come to a series of ledges with flamethrowers on them. Start heading up. When you get to the top, turn right, but don't jump over the block. The Enforcer is getting ready to attack. Now here's a sweet guy. He flies around with a rocket pack and blasts at you. To beat him, crouch down behind the block when he fires. After he fires he swoops down and around the screen. When he gets down near you, let him have a taste of Dirk.

Keep moving to the right, then take a long drop. Don't worry, unless Batman falls on something, he won't get hurt. Right after the long drop you'll meet a guy leaning up against the wall. Go to work on him right away, unless you like ninja stars and swordplay.

The boss of level 1 is the Killer Moth. He fires a four-way fireball at you. Stay on the left side of the pillar by the front door of City Hall. Be patient. He fires only from this one position, so wait for him to come down on your level—then blast him.

Level 2 takes you into the chemical factory. Stay out of the soup or you won't make it. Watch out for the drips of acid falling from the ceiling. Speaking of ceilings, this is where you meet Drop Claw. He is a genetic mutant blob on the ceiling that drops little mechanical claws that come after you and explode.

Go right, then up, then left across the platforms and decks above the chemical vats. The vats are full of Gluk which is a by-product of DDID—the stuff that puts the smile on the Joker's face! Don't fall in—it'll suck the life out of you.

Next, you reach two platforms on top of each other with a long jump to the right. To get past here without falling in the Gluk, jump down onto the side of the top platform and then jump to the right. It's a tricky move, but hey, you're Bat-man.

In 2-1 you meet the cannon with the grappler arm. Treat it like a flamethrower.

When you reach the back wall made up of green squares, start climbing up the left side of the platforms. Watch out for the electrical conduits. From this point on you have to be careful about how high you jump. When you get to the top, move right and jump between the rows of gears.

Master Tips

❏ The boss of level 2 is actually a mechanical room. Dodge the fire from the cannons on the right wall. Blast them and jump up on the conveyer belt. Watch out for the acid drips as you blast at the blue sensor in the upper left corner of the room. This shuts the electricity off in the upper right corner. Jump up there and get close to the cannons. When they come out to fire, crouch down against the wall under the blast. Then stand up and punch out the blue sensor. You will have to repeat this a few times.

❏ In levels 3 and 4 the Jader is a real pain in the neck. Run so that he's half on and half off the screen. When you have him like this, he can only jump up and down. Pick him off with the weapon of your choice.

❏ Punch the tanks on level 3. Your weapons aren't much good.

❏ To beat the Electrocutioner, jump up behind him to stay away from his electric personality. Punch him in the back of the head and he'll go away.

Blaster Master

Manufacturer: *Sunsoft*

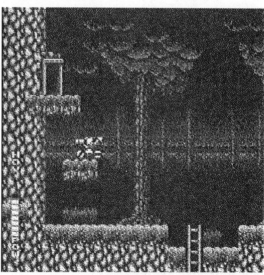

Up Front

Jason is a young fellow who has a pet frog called Fred. One day Fred, who wants only to get back to his pond, jumps out of his fish bowl and makes a mad dash for the door.

Jason sees Fred hopping across the yard and goes chasing after him. Fred's heading for the old radioactive chest that's rotting in the back yard. Before Jason can grab Fred, his nose bumps the chest and Fred gets showered with killer rads of plutonium dust. He transforms into a giant, mutant frog.

At just that moment, the ground opens up and swallows Fred, Jason, and the chest. After a long fall, and a big bump on the head, Jason wakes up to find the chest missing and Fred gone. Beside him is the wildest vehicle ever constructed, capable of blasting its way through hordes of killer mutants.

Jason decides to take off after the Evil Plutonium Boss to get Fred back. Happens in your neighborhood all the time, right?

Some of the best graphics work in this game was done with the armored vehicle. You'll notice how realistic the vehicle is as the wheels spin and the chassis flexes. The folks that created this game put a lot of work into it, and you are going to have to put a lot of play into it to beat it.

Getting Started

To beat this beauty of a shoot 'em up you'll have to master the eight levels of an underground labyrinth. The doorways to different levels make you go back through areas you've already conquered. You have to blast mutant monsters into the great beyond as you find your way through caverns and sewers and under some heavy water full of mutant jellyfish and swimming monsters. Many of these mutants are so happy to be out of their misery that they'll leave you generous power-ups, mostly energy.

Your vehicle can get you through most of this terrain. And your turret-mounted cannon can cut its way through most of the enemies. Blast everything in sight with deadly balls of fire. When Jason is in the vehicle, use these controls to move him around and blast the enemy:

$\updownarrow\!\!\blacktriangleleft\!\!\blacktriangleright$ Maneuver the vehicle over the rough terrain.

Ⓐ   Make the vehicle jump. Use the arrow controls in combination with A for real control.

Ⓑ   Fire your weapons!

Special weapons are available when you find the symbol for their power-up:

Homing missiles—These roam around the screen until they find an enemy to home in on.

Thunder Break—This fires bolts of lightning at enemies who are beneath you.

Multi-warheads—These fire three missiles at once.

Press Start to select the weapon you want. The numbers under the weapons show how many of each you have. Use the arrows to select a weapon, then press the Start button again to return to play. To fire these weapons, hold down the arrow button and press button B.

Sometimes Jason has to abandon his vehicle to get into places where the vehicle can't go. In fact, the first tip on this game is to try to get Jason into every nook and cranny where the vehicle can't go. Use these controls to move Jason when he's out of the vehicle:

Select   Get out of the vehicle and walk around.

Ⓐ   Fire a hand-held weapon.

Ⓑ   Toss hand grenades.

Moving On

As you progress through the stages, you collect different weapons that make you stronger or let you get into different places that you couldn't go before. Here's a list:

Crusher (Stage 1)—More powerful cannon.

Hyper (Stage 2)—You can crush some walls.

Hover (Stage 3)—You can float up higher than before.

Key (Stage 4)—Opens Door.

Dive (Stage 5)—Underwater swimming.

Wall I (Stage 6)—Wall climbing ability.

Wall II (Stage 7)—Drive across the ceiling.

You begin in Stage 1 where you fell. Move to the right and don't fall off the ledge unless you like explosions. If you do fall, jump back up as quick as you can. Don't roll!

In Stage 1 you meet enemies in radioactive suits— they'll try to jump on the vehicle and steal your power. You also meet flying whirligigs who try to knock you down.

When you get to places where the vehicle can't go, get out and explore. Walk into rooms, then blast the shrubs and some of the stones. Under these you will find power-ups. In fact, only rooms like this contain power-ups for your three special weapons.

When you move to a different part of the room and come back, all of the areas you blasted that were off the screen are restored. You can blast them all again, but the power-ups aren't there. Remember where you've been so you don't waste ammo. If you go totally out of the area, back to the vehicle, and enter again the power-ups will be restored too.

During your travels you will hear beeping sounds. You're getting close to some land mines. Don't run over them. If you shoot a mine, watch out for flying shrapnel.

The boss at the end of Stage 1 is a big red brain. Get inside the circle of floating cells and blast away with hand grenades. When you defeat the brain, you get Crusher, making your cannon more powerful.

To get to Stage 2, find the head on the wall that blows fire balls out of its mouth. You can only pass if you have Crusher.

As you enter Stage 2, move to the left, drop off the edge, and float downwards. There's a trap in the bottom right level of this screen. Here's the trick to get out: Come close to the ledge, point the turret to the opposite side, then jump and press the left arrow in one motion. It takes some practice, but you can do it. You'll see similar traps throughout the mazes.

In Stage 2 you meet the "little guys" for the first time. No matter how hard you try, you can't blast these guys with the cannon, unless you're below them and can jump up. Try to outrun them, jump up above them, use Thunder Break, or jump out of the vehicle and blast them by hand. This last method can be risky, but it's very effective.

See Advanced Information for a tip on how to beat the boss in Stage 2. You get Hyper when you complete Stage 2. This lets you blast through walls made up of small bricks.

Stage 3 is a mechanical world. Several new mutant buddies attack as you deal with cannons blasting at you from the ceiling and pods that drop red little guys on you—blast the pods before they open. If you thought the other little guys were a pain in the neck, wait till you see how hungry these guys are.

Stage 3 also brings you into contact with the Helmet Heads who spit rolling time-delay bombs at you. Then they come after you. To get by these guys, jump up even to where they are to attract their attention, but don't jump up onto their platform unless you have lots of room. When the balls go up, stay back until after they explode, then get ready to blast Helmet Head himself.

The boss in Stage 3 is a real pip—a big stone block that makes copies of himself and leaves them behind. You can only blast the colored block. When it turns brownish red, blast the next duplicate. The blocks throw all sorts of things at you—the worst of them is the laser fire. Stand in line with the corner of the block to avoid this little bit of nastiness. Eventually you'll get the upper hand and the blocks will start to disappear. After you blast the last one, you can hover above the ground.

Master Tips

❏ The instruction book leaves out maps to Stages 4 and 5. We'll help you a bit with Stage 4. To get into Stage 4 you need almost a full charge of Hover. Remember where all those H power-ups were? Go get some and play with Hover a little. Hold down the up arrow during a jump —flames appear at the wheels and keep you climbing. Go back to where the game started and use Hover to reach the ledges above.

❏ Stage 4 is an underground sewer system with many chambers that look exactly alike. At the bottom of one of these areas is a pipe and a crevice. Get the vehicle through the crevice to find the mutant boss.

❏ In many Stages there's a trick that you can use to defeat the boss. Toss a hand grenade and wait for it to explode. Press Start at just the right moment to pause the action—the grenade will continue to go off and defeat the boss even though the game is paused. Of course, this is kind of risky. If you're being hit when you press Start, you will be the one who suffers a large amount of damage.

❏ The mutant bosses are usually holed up in the farthest reaches of the Stage, but visit all of the doors—you never know where you might find one.

❏ When you leave your vehicle, you get back all of your energy when you return to it. This is especially handy when you're running low on energy and can't find an energy power-up.

Fester's Quest

Manufacturer: *Sunsoft*

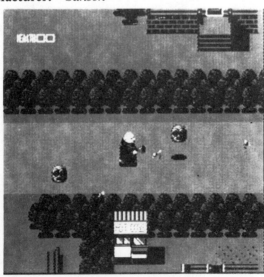

Up Front

Uncle Fester is up on the roof at night, wearing shades and enjoying a nice frog julep when he sees a UFO land in the city. Luckily for the city, when the aliens scanned the Addams house, they found no sign of life and left them unharmed. Here's Fester's chance to be a hero. Can Fester save the citizens of the city? Can he still light a bulb by sticking it in his mouth?

Getting Started

There isn't much to working the controller for this game:

⬆⬇◀▶	Move around the screen.
Ⓑ	Use the gun or his whip. If you have turbo firing mode, use it!
Ⓐ	Activate any of several items you collect along the way.
Start	Display a menu of the items and how many of each Fester has.
Select	Pause the action.

When Fester starts out, he has only a gun for a weapon. As you blast the aliens into kingdom come, many will leave behind items. Some of these items are power-ups and some of them are power-downs.

 Begin by blasting the little space globs that litter the street. Many of these give you different power-ups, such as keys to open houses, light bulbs to light dark sewers, and money to buy hot dogs. A five-dollar hot dog refreshes your life meter.

Other items include blocks that say GUN and WHIP. The blue ones power up your weapon. Don't touch the red ones—they power down a weapon.

The gun has eight different levels of effectiveness. Power it up as soon as possible. Once you get the full gun though, be careful not to shoot red gun blocks—the blue ones are hard to find.

After you beat the first boss and visit Morticia, you get the whip. Until then it doesn't matter what kind of whip blocks you run over—they have no effect. Once you have the whip you can get up to four levels of power.

The gun can't shoot through barriers, but you can use the whip to do what the gun can't—smack enemies over walls and other obstacles. You can also use the whip to pick up items that are out of reach.

You can get other items from family members by going to the door and using a key. To do this, press Start and highlight the key, press Start again, then press A when the play screen returns. Pugsly, Thing, or another member of the family will give you some useful items.

Moving On

You begin the game on a dead-end street. Move to the right and blast the space globs for items. When you get to the corner, go down until you get to the frogs, then turn around and come back up. The globs will have regrown and you can milk them for lots of power-ups. Once you have a few power-ups on the gun, try your hand at frog blasting. Instead of turning around when you see the red frogs at the bottom of the street, keep moving and work your way to the right.

Frogs are everywhere you go—each type has a unique feature. Blue frogs are easy to blast, red ones are the next easiest. Toughest of all are the green frogs. Some frogs start blue and then change colors as they jump toward you. As they get closer it takes more blasts to defeat them. Some red frogs spit fiery stingers at you. If you get hit, you will slow down to half speed until you pull the stinger out with the vice grips that Wednesday gives you.

If you stand in one place for very long, enemies will start coming at you in a continuous stream. This is when turbo blast comes in very handy. Moving the enemies off screen does not always clear a path. And since the stream keeps coming, it doesn't do much good to stand there and shoot. March straight into the stream with your gun blazing (on turbo if you have it). Keep moving!

Once you have a fully charged gun and some other items, move on. Come down the street and move to the left.

The floating heads are full of larvae that will quickly hatch into mosquitoes if you shoot them. If you shoot one, shoot the larvae and mosquitoes before you get stung. If you get stung, you're back to half-speed till you can get those vice grips from Wednesday.

Take the first opening between the hedges—go up and to the left. If you've been hit, buy a hot dog to fill your life meter. Walk up to the stand, select money on your menu and then press A when you go back to the game screen.

By now you should have several keys. Go to both of the houses. Pugsly will give you TNT and Wednesday will give you vice grips.

There's a set of steps near the first house. After you visit the second house, come back here. Choose light bulbs from the menu, stand over the steps, and press A to go down. (A lets you go up and down stairs.)

As soon as you're in the tunnel, move just a bit to get away from the stairs and press A to light the place up. Here in the underground tunnels and sewers, you meet several different alien enemies, mostly frogs. The mosquito heads are here, and sometimes you have no choice but to blast them as they block the path.

The most interesting creature here is the slime. This little green puddle of goo comes after you. When you blast it with your gun, it splits and multiplies. You can get lots of items from these guys, but they will also put down a lot of red gun blocks. Avoid these at all cost, even if you have to stand and blast a steady stream of enemies until the block disappears. Blast them in short bursts—the slimes will spread out, making it easier for you to pick up items without getting a red gun.

When you come out of the other end of the tunnel, you'll find yourself just across the crack in the street you saw before. On the right is a hot-dog stand. Go to the house on the left —Thing will give you potions to recharge your life meter. If you've been damaged, use one of the potions right away, then go back and get the potions again. You can only hold five, but you should have plenty of keys by now and one key for a recharge isn't a bad bargain.

Go back out and work your way up and to the left to the white building. Inside, you'll have your first experience with the 3-D view inside of buildings. Walk into a dead end corridor to get an extra bar on your life meter. Later you'll meet bosses behind the doors in these buildings.

Once you have the extra bar for your life meter, go to the right of the building. Go to the house in the upper left—Thing will give you Invisibility Potions. These potions make you invincible for about ten seconds. Come back, go down the path through the hedges, and take the stairs into the sewer.

When you get through this tunnel, you find another office building. Behind one of the doors in this building is the first boss.

This guy has long arms that whip out at you. Go to the lower left corner of the room. Step up between his arms and start blasting. He'll start moving to the right of the screen and try to hit you. Move with him before he starts hitting again. If you have a full power gun, this guy will be history before you get to the right side of the screen. Don't worry about wasting your potions—if you beat him you get all of them back.

Use TNT and invisibility potions to defeat the second boss.

Master Tips

- ❏ To get away from the big crabs when your weapons power is low, run away and drop TNT as you go. Three bangs and you have deviled crab.
- ❏ Be careful with the whip—it's easy to pick up a power-down by mistake.
- ❏ The last three office buildings hold some tough bosses. To beat Mr. Thunderblade, a cute guy with ram's horns and a sharp sword, you'll need to use every weapon you can get your hands on.
- ❏ Use the noose to call Lurch—he'll help you out of a jam.
- ❏ Find the secret way through the bushes to the Addams Family mansion, and find a fourth bar for the life meter.

Gauntlet

Manufacturer: *Tengen*

Up Front

The evil Morak has stolen the Sacred Orb and locked it in a vault, somewhere in the five worlds. You must find the clues that will give you the combination to the vault.

Within the five worlds are about a hundred rooms you must search through. As you search the rooms, your life meter counts down continuously, even if you don't get hit by one of the hordes of enemies. Each room is an elaborate maze containing power-ups and clues—you need to move fast.

Getting Started

You can play this game in any of three ways. In the one-player mode you're on your own. In two-player mode you and a friend can either compete or cooperate. You can also choose any of four different fighting characters, each with a different set of attributes:

Merlin	The wizard is strong in magic, but has little defensive skill.
Questor	This guy is an elf. Like most elves he is quick and nimble, but he's just a touch weak. One advantage he has, though, is that he can get to places where the others can't.
Thor	A big, burly warrior. Thor has the greatest strength of the characters, but he's slow. He's good for beginners, because he has the longest life line of all the characters.
Thyra	Thyra is a Valkyrie, a female warrior, and is known for all-around strength. This character is well-balanced, probably the second best fighter after Thor.

By the end of the game, power-ups even out each of the characters, so that you can beat this game with any of the four characters. You'll have to develop a slightly different strategy for each, however. The controls are fairly simple:

⬍◀▶   Move around the screen.

Ⓐ   Fire your weapons.

Ⓑ   Cast spells and use other weapons.

When you press the Start button, a screen appears that tells you what magic spells you have. At the bottom of the screen is a password that lets you continue the game when you get done in. This password only gets you as far as the first 78 rooms. If you get killed off after that, you need to start over.

Power-ups include extra portions of armor, speed, and other stuff that evens out the characters' capabilities as the game goes on. You can also get temporary power-ups that give you invulnerability, invisibility, super weapon strength, and a repulsion spell that makes all enemies run away from you.

Moving On

As you go through the mazes, collect all of the keys you can find. They open doors that you can't open any other way. Enemies are usually grouped inside of rooms. Often you'll find a skull and crossbones symbol among the enemies. Destroy this symbol—otherwise, the enemies continue to reproduce.

Collect as many items as you can, but remember that time is against you. Food items give you more life.

When you find a jug marked XXX, you can drink it or let it be. Some jugs have food value and will add 100 points to your life. Others contain poison—you'll lose 100 points.

Each room contains one or more places marked EXIT. This is the only way out of a room. When you exit a room, you'll see a map of the world that you're exploring. Make sure you visit all the rooms marked with a ?.

Along the way you'll find treasure rooms for you to explore. Not only do these rooms have a great number of treasures, but when you exit to go to the next room, you get recharged.

Watch out for glowing squares on the floor. If you step on one, you'll get stunned for a few seconds—the enemies will swarm all over you.

Cracked blocks crumble when shot. This is sometimes the only way into an area. Watch out also for trap doors. Walls aren't always what they seem to be.

Master Tips

❑ Check your time when you go into a treasure room, then find the exit. Once you know where the exit is, leave a trail of breadcrumbs so you can find your way back. Grab as much treasure as you can.

❑ You need all of the clues in the ? rooms to get into the vault.

❑ Chances are that the best exit to a room with more than one exit is the hardest one to get to.

Ironsword: Wizards and Warriors II

Manufacturer: *Acclaim*

Up Front

The Evil Wizard Malkil is at it again in the Land of Sindarin. In your last encounter (Wizards and Warriors I) you, Kuros, defeated Malkil, but your happily ever after is just about ready to come to an end.

Malkil has put an evil enchantment on the four Elementals—Wind, Fire, Earth, and Water. Each guards a fragment of the broken Ironsword. Your mission—conquer the Elementals, reunite the pieces of the sword, and do battle with the Evil One himself.

In Ironsword, Wizards and Warriors II you go mountain climbing through several different areas. Each of the areas is ruled by a different Elemental and is infested with different enemies. In each area you'll meet an Animal King who will help you when you bring him the right object. Along the way you'll find and buy many different objects, magical spells, and weapons that will help you do your job. You won't be able to use many of the objects, but they'll rack up the bonus points.

Getting Started

The controller for this game is simple:

◀▶	Move left and right across the screen.
▼	Crouch and duck.
Ⓐ	Jump. For more control over the jump, hold down button A and press the left or right arrow.
Ⓑ	Control your sword or other weapon.
▲ Ⓑ	To stab at things over your head, hold down the up arrow and press button B.

Press Select to call up the Magic screen. Here you will select which magic spells to use and find your current password. Since the game offers only a limited number of continues, write down your password whenever you get a major power-up. If you get knocked off, you can enter the password and restart at the previous level.

Each of the Elementals is vulnerable to a special kind of magic spell. To succeed you should follow the Seven Noble Steps of Sindarin:

1. Obtain keys.
2. Unlock treasure chests to find magic.
3. Obtain the golden object.
4. Take the golden object to the Animal King.
5. Pass into the Elemental's area and find the right magic.
6. Defeat the Elemental with magic.
7. Take another fragment of the Ironsword.

You begin your quest at the foot of the mountain. Just below the playing portion of the screen is a status area that tells you about your current condition. On the left side of the screen is a run-down of the following items:

Score	How many points you've racked up.
Money	How many gold coins you have for buying things.
Life	How much life force you have. If the meter is zero, you die.
Magic	You must have magic power as well as the spell before you can cast a spell.

The swords in the middle of the screen indicate the number of lives you have. On the right of the screen you will see an inventory of the items you've found, a count of the keys you have, and a picture that tells you what Elemental you're fighting.

Moving On

In the first level of the game you do battle with the Wind Elemental. First, however, you must find the Golden Egg and take it to the Eagle King. He will take you into the clouds where you will complete the second half of this level.

Climb the mountain by jumping from ledge to ledge. Fight off the birds and the other creatures that come after you.

As you climb, you will almost certainly stumble and fall. Notice the diagonal slopes that are a part of the mountain's design. When you miss a jump, you'll slide down these slopes until you land on a ledge. Be careful when you jump—you could slide way down and have to start over. You'll have to deal with this "Chutes and Ladders" stuff throughout the game.

You'll encounter many secret doors in this game. You come to one near the top of the mountain where there's a single ledge on the edge of the water.

As you climb the mountain, investigate every door you come to. Some of these doors are treasure rooms, some are traps, and some are inns. When you come across an inn, you can buy keys and weapons, food and magic, but you must have the cash. If you're short of money, you can try the Bonus Chance. You risk 100 gold coins, but you might win 290. On the menu of the inn is the choice, Bonus Chance. Select this choice and highlight the cup that you think the skull will land on. If you're right, you win. If you're wrong, you're broke.

Get the Golden Egg. The direct approach is the hardest. Go above the place where the egg lies, and come down to it—this way is a lot easier. Once you have it, work your way up and to the left to find the Eagle King—he'll take you to meet the Wind Elemental.

Here, you need to find the helmet, the Book of Sindarin, and the WindBane Spell. Without the spell, you won't have a chance against the Elemental boss. You can jump higher by holding down the A button. Keep A down and you'll start bouncing as though you're on a trampoline.

Make sure you have a key with you when you go after the WindBane Spell. The little green guys who spit feathers at you are deadly. You wouldn't want to have to come in here twice.

To beat the old blowhard, you will have to stab at the projectiles coming from his eyes. Use the WindBane and keep stabbing.

The next Elemental is Water. In this level you need to collect the shield, the water spout, and the Golden Fly. Take the Golden Fly to the Frog King. The water spout spell is a special bit of magic that takes you high up into places you couldn't otherwise reach. Don't go to the Frog King without the Golden Fly or you'll lose the spell.

Once you've delivered the fly, the king will let you into the underwater world of the Elemental. Move left and jump down the waterfall. Go under water and to the right. Can you walk through walls?

Master Tips

❏ Magic power is often hidden in some pretty unlikely places. Try jumping up into dead-end ceilings, especially if they come to a point.

❏ Some of the doors in the Fire level are shortcuts back to lower places on the mountain. Check them all out anyway. Just remember which ones took you back, and don't go into them again. Make yourself a map.

❏ When you get to the cave where the Crown is hidden, you'll see a slide that forks at the bottom. Use Fleet Foot to make the slide to the right. Without it you will fall to the left—away from the good stuff.

❏ To get the Gauntlet to give the Bear King, go to the cliff and jump up, hitting the wall to loosen the Gauntlet.

❏ Once you have beaten the Elementals, you have one more mountain to climb. You have to beat the Elementals again to make it to the evil, mean, and nasty one himself.

Ninja Gaiden

Manufacturer: *Tecmo*

Up Front

The Oriental fight 'em ups have come to your local Nintendo system in the guise of Ninja Gaiden. While many of the Nintendo games have simple plots that merely hold the action together, Ninja Gaiden provides a more detailed story in movie-like form. In fact, the Ninja Gaiden story has six parts.

The plot is laid out for you in a series of scenes. You play the role of the hero, Ryu, and fight your way through to the next scene. Along the way you are treated to a devilishly delightful and challenging game.

Getting Started

The story begins as young Ryu's father, also a master Ninja, does battle with an unknown assailant. Against the backdrop of the full moon, we see his father defeated. The next morning, Ryu finds a letter from his father instructing him to take the heirloom Dragon Sword to America and find his father's old friend Walter Smith.

The basic controls for this game are simple and straightforward although some of the control combinations get a bit complex:

⬍◆◗	Move Ryu around and about the screen.
Ⓑ	Swing your sword.
Ⓐ	Jump for it!

Of course, next to a New York cat burglar, no one can work walls like a Ninja. You'll have to develop some climbing skills before you can get very far with this game.

Many places in the game have walls close enough together that Ryu can work his way to the top by way of the Wall Climb. When Ryu jumps onto a wall, he can hang on to the spot where he lands. Press button A to make him jump, then press the arrow key towards the target wall to make him spring to the opposite wall. You can climb many places using this technique.

Ryu can also attack from his perch on the wall. Press button B while springing down from a wall for an effective method of lunging at enemies from a relatively safe place.

You may not time a jump correctly and end up landing on the side of a wall instead of on the top as you had planned.

This is a tricky situation to get out of. A joystick is helpful here, but not absolutely necessary. To climb back up when there is no wall opposite to spring to, push the arrow button away from the wall, then jump. Quickly push the arrow button back in the direction of the wall. Use this technique to save Ryu from plummeting into the abyss.

At the top of the screen is a status area that shows how many points you have and how much time you have left to complete the level. It also shows the weapons you have and two graphs showing Ryu's strength and the strength of the boss you must defeat at the end of each act.

To begin, Ryu's graph shows all red. As he's hit by various enemies, his strength is sapped. When all the red is gone, so is Ryu. Just below his strength meter is a graph showing the strength of the enemy. This meter only comes into play at the end of each act. Each time you strike the enemy boss, he loses some of his strength. When the red is gone, so is the boss.

Don't be overly concerned about the time display. You have more than enough time to complete the mission. If you get close to the end of the level, stay and fight a little longer to get points.

 In each act (level) you'll find lanterns or candles hanging on the wall. Slash at them with the sword. You can get a lot of treasures by doing this. Among the treasures are bonus points, 1-ups, and power boosts, as well as the red bag that restores Ryu's energy.

Mixed in with the treasures are Ninja weapons—small throwing stars, windmill throwing stars (they act like boomerangs), the Fire Wheel that makes Ryu temporarily invulnerable, the Art of the Fire Wheel which lets Ryu throw fire at enemies, and the ability to jump and slash. Jump and slash is a particularly effective weapon because it lets Ryu jump and spin, making his sword act like a saw. This is particularly useful for jumping down on opponents from above.

These weapons don't come free, and you can only use one at a time. When you slash a lantern, the symbol for one of the weapons may fall to the ground where you can pick it up. Pick it up, and it takes the place of the previous weapon. The small throwing stars cost three points when you use them, all other weapons cost you five points. Don't let that worry you either. The idea is to come back alive. Points are nice to have, but you can't take 'em with you.

Moving On

Your quest begins in the town of Galesburg. This part of the game is short—it gives you a chance to warm up before the real action begins. As you move to the right across the screen, different enemies attack you—anything from street punks to guys who think they're Mike Tyson. Beware of the Dogmen. To beat these guys crouch (using the down arrow) and slash low. These guys are pesky. While you're here, practice the Wall Climb and the Wall Spring maneuvers—you'll need them later. Slash the lanterns to find out what is where.

Throughout the game you find out where your favorite weapons are stashed. Try making a map.

After this short tune up, you come to a door at the end of the street. Here, you meet your first boss—the evil Barbarian. Stay away from his ax. He slashes at you in bursts. When he stops to prepare for another attack, move in and whack him a few times. The enemy meter in the status area will show you how close you are to doing him in.

Once you defeat the Barbarian, the movie plays a little bit more of the plot. Who is this girl? Why does she have a gun?

In Act II you wake to find yourself in a dungeon. Surprise! The girl is springing you from your jail cell and giving you a wild looking statue.

Here you go again. You must fight your way out of the Outpost and make your way up into Death Valley. Can you get any lower than this? Yes, if you miss a jump and go through one of the spaces in the floorboards, you'll never be heard from again.

If you can make it through these scenes, you wind up at Amura's Alter, home of the Bomberman. Bomberman is a lean, mean fighting machine. He swings a sickle on a chain, and it's deadly! Fortunately for you he's not too bright. Wait till he comes for you, then jump on the wall. He continues to swing his chain low as if you were pinned against the wall (a place you definitely don't want to be!), jump over his head and whack him from behind. When he turns to get you, run to the other wall and repeat the moves.

Act III takes you through Crystal Lake and the Lizard Mountains to Yomi's Cave. Along the way you meet a whole new class of nasties. Pay special attention to the Eagles— they're a real pain, a deadly pain.

There's a 1-up in 4-1, but you need to get the slash and jump to get it. You'll come to a place where you can take the high road or the low road. Go high. The first spider on the wall hides the slash and jump. Once you have it go back and take the low road. You meet two spiders. Don't get the one just before the soldier with the gun—it will take away your slash and jump. Take out the soldier, then slash and jump the second spider. This is in an awkward position—that's why you need the slash and jump.

Another 1-up is hidden in 4-2. You'll come to an area with a short section of elevated mine cart track. Take the low path and slash the lanterns to once again get the jump and slash. Now all you have to do is jump up onto the high path and slash the lantern on the left to get another life.

The boss at the end of Act IV is actually two bosses, but one of them is a phantom. The Kelbeross will jump about and spit deadly bubbles at you. You can only hurt one of them, but either one can hurt you. Stay near the left pedestal and slash at the one whose jumps are longer and stronger—stay away from his brother.

The final act takes place in the inner shrine of the temple ruled by Jaquio. The fighting gets frenzied, but there is nothing really new here until . . . . To tell you too much more might spoil the movie for you. All we can tell you is that the first boss you must fight at the end of this section is one bad dude—you don't want to fight this guy. Slash at the icon on the back wall to win the day. When fighting the second boss, go for the eye.

Master Tips

❏ Make the most of the unlimited continues.
❏ If you've already seen the movie part of the game, you can use the Start key to bypass the dialogue.

❏ When the date screen is displayed, hold down left arrow, down arrow, button A, button B, and the Select buttons, then press Start to cycle through the sound effects used in the game. Each has a number. Pressing the A will play them for you. It doesn't really do anything to help you beat the game, but it's fun.

River City Ransom

Manufacturer: *Technos*

Up Front

Gangs of thugs, punks, and bullies, dirt balls of every description, all under the command of the gang lord, Slick, have taken River City High School hostage. Since there aren't any cops in River City (at least not at the high school), the fate of the school lies in the hands of Alex and Ryan, two clean cut American kids with advanced karate/kung fu skills. Ryan has a special reason for fighting his way through the gangs. His girlfriend is one of the hostages.

Getting Started

When you first start the game, you need to give Alex and Ryan names to use for the rest of the game. Then, choose to play with one or two players. You're given twenty dollars and transported to the sidewalk in front of the high school. This is where you'll start to take on gangs and groups of gangs along with ten or so bosses to earn the right to confront Slick.

Before you can start fighting, set the speed at which messages are displayed to either slow, normal, or fast. Then, choose the skill level—novice or advanced. If you find that you've chosen the wrong skill level, don't worry, you can change it during the game.

At any time during the game you can press Start to bring up a menu that lets you check or change several different things:

Belongings	Once you acquire items, they are stored here. Come to this part of the menu to use them.
Level	This part of the menu lets you adjust the message speed and the skill level. The advanced level presents you with many more enemies to fight.
Status	This screen shows the abilities and condition of the fighting characters in numeric form.
Help	This menu item explains how to use the menu system.
Password	This game uses long and complex passwords. Come here to write down your password after defeating bosses or gaining important items. Come here also to resume an old game.

Use Select to change your stamina meter into a money counter and back again.

The moves in this game are pretty complex, but they give you a lot of control. Four pages of the instruction booklet are taken up in explaining them. Here are a few highlights:

⬍⬌	Move around the screen. Make sure you're in the right position or your punches won't reach the bad guys. (To sprint, choose a direction and press that arrow button twice quickly.)
Ⓐ	Punch when you have no weapon. Use a weapon if you have one. (If you pick up an enemy, you can use him as a weapon.)
Ⓑ	Kick. (If you have a weapon or enemy in hand, press B to throw it.)
ⒶⒷ	Press A and B together to jump.
ⒶⒷ	Press either button to pick up items or enemies. Get near and press A or B. If the enemy is standing on a weapon, you will pick up both.

Moving On

You start out on the sidewalk in front of River City High School. Walk to the right. Almost immediately, several members of the local gang welcome you. As you kick and punch, you will notice that they drop their change where you can get it. Pick it up—you'll need it to buy food, items, and other stuff to keep you alive. After all, everybody's got to eat.

When thugs come at you with weapons, punch or kick them. They'll drop their weapons—pick up the weapon you want; you can use it as long as you want, as long as you can drag it from screen to screen. You can only have one weapon at a time.

When you get to the trash pick-up area, some of the local trash will attack you. Pick up cans and use them as weapons. You can also kick items like the trash cans into your enemies to inflict damage.

Head down the alley to the Grodo mall where you can buy food to recharge your stamina meter. When you buy items, they add up to give you increased strength. Keep an eye on the status screen to see what you can do. Food items concentrate on stamina. Other items give you capabilities plus some stamina too.

Get $26.95 in your pocket before you go into the store with the blue and white awnings. Buy the Dragon Feet to increase your kicking ability.

After you leave the mall, you come to a red area between two posts. This is the park. Go past it now, but remember where it is. You will come back here to fight a boss.

Watch out for the missing roadway in the second trash pick-up area. Don't fall in the hole. Stay on the sidewalk.

The first boss you'll meet is in the warehouse. You'll have to take on a few guys to get to him, but some of these guys are really dumb. Go up and left, then go to the door on the other side.

This boss goes by the name of Rocko. If he hits you, you'll know it, but he's easy to knock down. Don't let him get set when he gets back up or you'll get nailed. Keep banging on him every time he gets up and he's a goner.

Now, go get Blade in the park.

Master Tips

❑ Ask for the free smile in Merv's Burger Joint to get special treatment. Blush Blush!

❑ If one of the bad guys throws rocks at you when you have the lead pipe weapon, play ball!

❑ To beat the Dragon Twins, make sure you have a good supply of vitamins (to recharge stamina)—their flying spin kicks suck the life right out of you. Stay on them and don't let them off the screen—they come back with with weapons. Grand Slam is handy to have here too.

❑ Acro Circus makes you as nimble as a circus acrobat, and twice as hard to hit.

❑ Some of the tougher bosses give you lots of money. You can always go back in and fight them again to pile up cash in a hurry.

❑ Don't jump on gym equipment and basketball stuff, unless you can't find any other way out.

❑ The best way to win this game is to power up. Beat up all the lower level thugs and punks to get money to buy enough power items. These will help you get through the final portions of the game.

Strider

Manufacturer: *Capcom*

Up Front

The plot to this game is really dumb. The only thing it has going for it is that it doesn't send you on a quest to rescue a fair princess. Thankfully, the game is not dumb. It has some unusual action and settings. The graphics are good, and the action is tough.

Strider is "the strongest secret maneuvers group in the world." They make the Delta Force and the Green Berets seem like Boy Scouts. An average Strider is the equal of an entire team of special forces.

Hiryu, your character in the game, was the youngest top level Strider ever. After performing a particularly nasty piece of business, he retired to Mongolia. But now his friend, Kain, has been captured by the enemy. Matic, the Vice-Director of Strider, appears on Hiryu's doorstep to tell him the bad news. Matic demands that Hiryu return to the force and eliminate Kain. Under the threat of mass slaughter of his neighbors, Hiryu sets out to find Kain, not to kill him, but to rescue him.

After rescuing his friend, he finds out that there's a lot of evil, mean, nasty stuff going on, and that there's something rotten in Strider. As you might guess, he goes after the entire organization. Whether he wins or not is up to you. Keep track of your passwords so that you can continue tomorrow. You must prevail!

Getting Started

All of the action of the game is centered around the Blue Dragon console. Hiryu must return here to move to the next area and to analyze information he finds on floppy disks.

The basic moves for the character are simple. As the game goes on, you acquire new strengths and moves:

- ◄►   Move Hiryu through the areas.
- ▼   Crouch and duck.

Ⓐ   Jump!

Ⓑ   Attack with the cipher (sword/spear). Use the up
            arrow to aim the cipher upward (this is handy
            for attacking enemies above you).

⬆Ⓑ   Later in the game Hiryu acquires the plasma
            arrow. To fire this weapon hold the up arrow for
            several seconds, then press B.

⬇Ⓐ   Later you acquire the slide move. Press the
            down arrow plus either left or right (depending
            on your direction) and hit A.

You gain speed going down ramps and slopes. Use this
speed to jump farther than normal. You can also climb walls
(as in Ninja Gaiden) by jumping from wall to wall and back
again, working your way up. You'll find some interesting
things up there.

Some doors are locked, some are not. For most doors
you only need the corresponding numbered key. You may want
to visit these areas more than once. Some doors open when
you've eliminated all of the enemies on the screen.

You can return to the console by going off the left edge
of the screen at the starting point of each location. Leave a
trail of breadcrumbs, or at least remember how to get back to
the starting point.

Moving On

You begin your adventure in Kazah. Move to the right and
infiltrate the building by way of the air shaft. Air shafts are a
large part of your transportation. Crouch down with the B button to go down one and jump to go up one. If the shaft has
arrows pointing in only one direction, you can travel only in
that direction.

As you go through this area, you encounter various Ninja
types who are kind of wimpy. It won't take long for you to get
a key and a disk.

As you fight your way to the left, you'll come to an opening in the beams. Jump right in, but press the right arrow
button as you fall to direct yourself to a safe landing spot.
When you press the left or right arrows while falling, you fall
to that side. If you fall straight down here, you'll have a rough
time with some spikes.

When you come to the air shaft, jump up. By this time you'll have the S-1 key, but the S-3 door won't open for you. Come back later.

Take the next air shaft up, then move to the right and down again. When you get to the bottom, come up and to the left again. You can attack from below with the cipher—press the up arrow and then jump.

As you work your way across this area, you'll come to many doors that don't require keys. Near these doors are air shafts. When enemies come after you from here, simply point the cipher up and stab them as they fall out of the shafts.

The mechanical enemies you meet here are easy if you stay back and don't let them punch you.

When you get to the big blue box, you will meet someone who gives you disk number two. Take both disks back to the Blue Dragon console to analyze them.

Master Tips

❑ Find the Aqua boots in Egypt. They will help you defeat sharks and let you walk on water. Use the wall climbing moves to get up to where they are.

❑ To beat the mad motorcyclist, jump up and turn, striking from behind.

❑ The final battle is with the Red Dragon himself, but before you can take him on you have to beat almost every enemy you have seen so far one more time.

Teenage Mutant Ninja Turtles

Manufacturer: *Ultra*

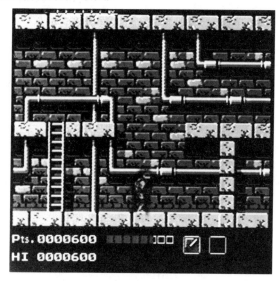

Up Front

Most parents can't even say Teenage Mutant Ninja Turtles, much less deal with the concept of four pizza slurping terrapins fighting through the streets of New York on the side of law and order. Get ready for Leonardo, Raphael, Michaelangelo and Donatello to take over your Nintendo just as they've taken over Saturday morning television.

In this game you must take on five different levels of action with five different plots (you guessed it, one of the five is rescuing the kidnaped damsel) before the big showdown with the evil Shredder in the Technodrome.

The neatest part of this game is that you have your choice of four turtles, each with his own favorite weapon and special skills:

Leonardo	A master swordsman. He's fast and strong, and his blade gives him a fairly long reach.
Raphael	He prefers the Sai, a very sharp, pointed dagger. His moves are precise and deadly.

Michaelangelo   A courageous nun'chuck kind of guy. In strength he is about on a level with Raphael. He does best in close-up battles when enemies are at his feet.

Donatello   The strongest of the bunch, he's a touch slower than the others. He makes up for his lack of quickness with his weapon, the bo, which is a really hefty stick.

You can switch back and forth from fighter to fighter any time you like. Each turtle has his own life meter. When that meter reaches zero, he is captured. You must go on without him until you get a chance to rescue him.

Getting Started

Since you have so many weapons and fighting techniques at your fingertips, the controls give you a lot of variety:

◆▶   Move around the screen turtle-style.

◆▼   Duck or aim upwards when you're watching the action from the side.

Ⓑ   Attack with the selected weapon.

Ⓐ   Jump.

ⒶⒷ   To jump and attack at the same time, press both at once. Leonardo becomes a flying Veg-o-matic with this move.

Select   Cycle among the weapons at your disposal.

In the third level, you inherit the Party Van. Steer with the arrows, fire the cannon with A, and let missiles rip with B.

 As you work your way through the various sewers and buildings of old New York, you'll come across many items. Whole pizzas will restore one turtle's life meter completely. Partial pizzas give partial relief. Other power-ups include ninja throwing stars in two different flavors, a boomerang, missiles, a rope, and each of the weapons carried by the guys. This lets you give Raphael Leonardo's sword. Ever wondered what Donatello would do with nun'chucks? Change characters before picking up the power-up to give it to the turtle you want to have it.

The status area under the play portion of the screen shows your score, today's high score, a life meter for your turtle, and any power-up weapons the turtle has. Some of these weapons have a limited capacity. The number below them is the number of shots you have left for that weapon.

If you pause the action with the Start button, you'll see another screen. On this screen you'll find a map and a clue area. The most important part of this area lets you use the arrow buttons to switch between the four characters.

Moving On

As the game begins, the Foot Clan, arch rivals of the TMNT gang, have kidnapped April the newscaster. You must save her.

When you first start out, compare your position on the map frequently to get the hang of knowing where you are. Some of the sewers look similar and you don't want to visit them twice.

When the game begins you're standing next to a manhole in the street on the north side of a building. This sewer only leads to the south side of the building. You will get little out of it except experience.

If this is your first try at the shell game, go in the tunnel and try on all the characters for size. At the other end of this tunnel is a slice of pizza. If you have a character who is low on energy, you can take him in and out of the tunnel until his life meter is full. Do this as many times as necessary for each character. It isn't as quick as a continue, but you won't lose weapons and points.

Once you're comfortable with things, forget that entrance and come around the left side of the building. Avoid the steamroller and move to the bottom of the building. Go two manhole covers to the right, and the adventure begins.

When you enter the second manhole, move quickly to avoid the flying nasties. At this point use whatever turtle you are comfortable with, but try to save Donatello for later.

Move to the right—you'll come to a wall. At this point you will see April on the top deck. Before you can help her, you have to deal with the mini-boss Bebop who is on the bottom deck with you. Get as far to the right as you can and let him come after you. He'll walk into the wall. If you can get behind him, keep whacking on him so that he doesn't have a chance to turn around—you can finish him off without losing any more life.

Quick! Rocksteady is taking off with April! Jump up and out of the manhole and run after them into the building. When you come in the door, notice the large pizza on the top floor. By the time you get there you'll need it. Donatello is a good choice here—he can fight enemies on the top floor while he stays on the bottom floor. Watch out for the roof leapers —they love to jump off the ceiling at you. Clean this place out. There is a mini-boss or two, but they aren't any harder than some of the foes you've already faced.

Come out of the building and make your way to the second manhole cover to the north of the building. Stay out of the other one unless you're searching for a captured turtle. About all you'll get in there is a funeral.

In the next tunnel you encounter the sleepers. Use their little naps to get position. Only Raph and Don can block their fire.

Go down into the manhole and start moving left. A second life meter shows up on the screen to announce that a mini-boss is on the way. Switch to Leo and get up on the ledge to the left of the floor. From this place you can hit the two-legged frog with the sword and not get hurt.

Get through this part of the sewer and go into the blue building. You have to deal not only with flying nasties, but with moving belts as well. Use Leo or Don for their extra reach. Stay on the top deck to avoid as much fighting as possible and get to the right end of the floor.

Move up one more floor and climb the hill of crates on the left. When you come over the top, move left to where April is. The boss shows up to see what's going on. Quick, jump back up on the crates and switch to Donatello. The boss will follow you right into the wall. All you have to do is hack at him from above—he can't get to you.

Master Tips

❏ In level 2, be careful of the dam. Where the railing is broken, dive into the water and defuse all eight bombs that have been set to blow up the dam.

❏ The underwater sequence here is really neat. You must avoid the electric beams and killer seaweed and beat the clock. You'd better have several fully charged turtles before going into this one.

❏ Certain weapons can go through floors and ceilings.

❏ If you throw a boomerang and switch characters before it returns, you can give the new character boomerang power.

❏ When a turtle is getting low on energy, you will hear a beeping noise as a warning. Switch to a different turtle before the meter runs completely out. If you get him out of action before he gets captured, you can feed him pizza later. Once he's captured you can't use him again until you find him. Only one place in each level has a rescue point.

❏ There's a place in level 5 that's guarded by soldiers with laser rifles. Stay low and move slow—they won't be able to touch you.

❏ Beware of walls with saw teeth—go slow.

❏ Throw stuff at the Technodrome Guardian. Pay attention to the doors too. Shredder is easy compared to him.

The Adventures of Bayou Billy

Manufacturer: *Konami*

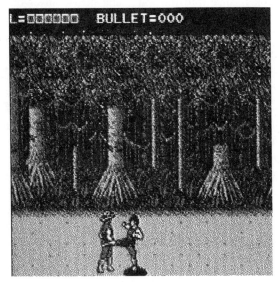

Up Front

Gordo, the gangster king of Bourbon Street, is ticked off. Because of you his Red Beans and Rice Warehouse is a smoking ruin. How's a crook going to get any smuggling done with his headquarters all a mess like that?

Of all the creatures in the swamp it is you, Bayou Billy, that Gordo fears the most. So he hatches a plan to kidnap your sweet honey, three-time cover girl for *Swamp Digest*, Annabelle, right off your front porch. Just your luck, for once his plans are a success.

Well, don't just stand there bellowing like a bull gator. It's off through the swamp and through the marshes of Cajun country as you attempt to rescue your sweet Annabelle from the grasp of Gordo.

Parents may not care for the way our buxom heroine is trussed up in her halter top and short shorts. The kidnapped heroine story is a little old. And many Southerners (even some of us transplanted Yankees) are offended by the backwoods stereotypes of the characters. In short, there's a lot to criticize in this game, but the challenge of the game is not one of them— 'taint no easy game.

It combines elements from several different styles of Nintendo games. You got car chases, hand-to-hand combat, light-gun compatible marksmanship, guns, knives, whips, and even ugly sticks to whap them ugly gators on the head. And none of it is easy.

Getting Started

When the title screen comes up, you get the chance to select the game you want to play. If you have the Nintendo Zapper, or some other light-gun, choose the A game. In the B game, you use the controller for shooting. You can also choose to go through a practice round for each of the three types of game play—racing, fighting, or shooting. You even have a choice to mess around with the game's sounds.

Your controller movements vary depending on what you're doing:

Fighting

⬍⬌	Move Billy around the screen. Line him up with the enemy you're trying to hit.
Ⓐ	Kick low.
Ⓑ	Punch or use a weapon that you've taken from one of your enemies.
ⒶⒷ	Do a flying kick. Get your timing right, and this is really effective.

Driving

⬍	Increase or decrease speed.
⬌	Steer the car.
Ⓐ	Toss dynamite at the attacking airplanes before they can drop bombs on you.
Ⓑ	Fire the machine gun.

Shooting

With Light-gun	In the shooting scenes, plug the light-gun into the slot for controller 2. Stand about six feet from the screen and go to it.

If you're playing the B game, your controller is the gun. Use the arrow keys to move the cross hairs around the screen.

Ⓐ   Fire the gun. You only have so many bullets, so make every shot count.

At the top of the screen is a status area. Each of the three different types of game play displays a different status area:

Fighting   The display shows your points, today's high score, the number of lives you have left, a life meter that shows how much damage you can stand, a bullet counter, and sometimes a life meter for bosses.

Driving   The display shows your speed, how much time is remaining, how many lives you have left, and a line with a flag on the right side and a symbol on the left that shows you how much of the course you have completed. The nearer the symbol is to the flag, the closer to the end of the level you are.

Shooting   The display shows your point totals, how many lives remain, a life meter, and how many bullets you have left.

Throughout the game you'll find different types of power-ups that you can either pick up and use, run over with the car, or shoot with the gun. Some of these are weapons. There is a gun, a throwing knife, a whip and the good ol' fashioned ugly stick. Most of the time you will have to knock weapons out of the enemy's hand then pick them up. Other power-ups include the following:

Meat—restores your life meter.

Bulletproof vest—helps to protect you from some weapons.

First aid box—restores your life meter.

Star—eliminates all enemies on the screen.

Gas cans—add extra time to the driving scenes.

Moving On

You begin your quest deep in the swamps where the men are men and the gators are hungry. Things start slowly enough as you engage some of Gordo's swamp rats in some good natured fun. Punch, kick, and claw your way through these goons. Make sure that your shadow is on a line with your enemy's shadow—otherwise, you'll be doing pretty moves but only hitting air.

Learn the jump kick well—it's your best move. If your enemy has weapons, take them away and use them on their owners.

Make your way to the creek. Forget the gators. Try to get across without fighting them. You'll have plenty of chances for some fresh gator meat before long. These guys just don't have a whole lot to offer you.

On the other side of the creek you'll have a whole lot of fun with rocks and sticks. Forget the rocks, unless one is heading through the air at you (you might want to duck)— grab the ugly stick and whack the guys after they throw the rocks.

Keep the stick from this battle, forget the knife in the next scene. After the knife-carrying dudes you'll be in gator country. Stand to the left of the logs. When one of these ugly lizards tries to come up out of the water at you, whack him with the ugly stick. As you whomp up on 'em, they give up meat that restores your life meter. Even though it disappears under water, you can get it when you wade through. The gators will swim back and pick it up before attacking you again, so even though you see four meat power-ups fall in the water, you'll only be able to collect one.

After you get by the gators, you'll meet some new friends. The one you want to get to know first is Whitey—he's got on a bulletproof vest that would look mighty fine on you. Not to mention that the other guys have guns. If you get by these boys, you'll have a gun and a few less bullets.

To end this level you have to make it past one more gator-infested swimming hole.

Stage 2 is a shooting stage. You are deep in the swamps and all kinds of bad guys are coming into view. You begin with

100 bullets. In addition to the moving targets, you can also get hold of a few different power-ups. The hourglass will stop your bullet meter. During the time that this power-up is active, you can't use any of the bullets shown on the status line.

The Star destroys all the enemies on the screen, and the bulletproof vest lessens the damage when you are hit. Have you ever been in a shooting gallery where the targets shoot back?

If you score enough points, this level ends with a wild helicopter shoot out. Contrary to some published reports, controllers with a slow motion option are a real help in downing the chopper.

Level 4 is the first of two driving stages. It is called I-10, the Road to New Orleans. Now friends, Interstate 10 runs right through the back yard of the city where I wrote this book. Your humble author has even driven it all the way to New Orleans—it has never been like this!

First of all, you're running against a clock as well as enemies—try to do over 150 mph. Bad guys shoot at you, poles on the side of the road seem to come out of nowhere, and smugglers in airplanes try to drop bombs on you. Up until now, Gordo has just been playing with Billy's mind!

Levels 4 and 5 are both driving levels. Level 5 is one or two notches higher on the difficulty scale than 4. This is where a lot of people get bogged down. It's tough, but all it takes is patience and practice. Start out slowly at first—you aren't going to make it through the first time anyway. Get a feel for the rhythm of the road. Practice your timing for hurling TNT at the airplanes.

Master Tips

❏ The boss at the end of Stage 3 is one real nasty dude —don't get too close or he'll toss you like a sack of grits. Stay back and jump kick, then get away.

❏ In certain places enemies flash red before they attack. If a character has his hands in his pockets, beware of sneak attacks. Keep your distance.

❏ Whips don't run out of bullets! A good whip is worth three guns in the city.

- ❑ Keep an eye out for two-legged rats under manhole covers.
- ❑ Smack that dude on the motorcycle!
- ❑ The closer you get to the end, the better armed your enemies will be. Remember to keep your distance, look in windows and in dark places. To defeat many of these enemies you have to knock them out of their bulletproof vests first. Collect as many of these vests as you can.
- ❑ Only five continues are available to you, so try to score high. A 1-up is awarded at the first 20,000 points, and every 30,000 after that.

The Uncanny X-men

Manufacturer: *LJN*

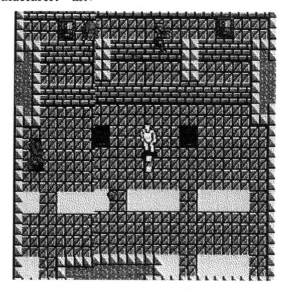

Up Front

The whole World is in an uproar! The evil Magneto, a truly electric villain, and his band of nasties is on the loose. World destruction is just around the corner. The only hope is Professor Xavier and his Uncanny X-men.

The heroes and villains of this game are straight from the pages of Marvel Comics. You know, those wonderful folks who brought you SpiderMan and Captain America.

In this game you can choose to fight with Wolverine, Storm (a girl!), Nightcrawler, Cyclops, or Iceman. Each of the fighters has a different mix of skills. Some are faster than others, some fight close, some can shoot from far away, while some can take more punishment than the rest. That's what makes this game so much fun.

Getting Started

Using the controller is the same no matter which character you're fighting with:

⬍◀▶	Move around the screen.
Ⓐ	Punch or fire.
Ⓑ	Jump or fly, depending on the character.
Start	Display the status screen. This is the only place you can see the life meters.
Select	Cycle between characters in the one-player mode.

When you choose the two-player mode, each fighter is assigned a separate controller. The one-player mode is unique because you still get two fighting characters. You control one and the computer controls the other. Press Select to take control of the other character. You will probably want to switch fairly often since the computer is not as good a player as you are. If the computer-controlled character gets too far behind, you won't be able to move off the screen.

You must complete four separate missions to succeed. You may perform them in any order you wish.

Moving On

This game is chock full of power-ups. There isn't a great variety, but they're all extremely useful:

Energy barrels—one of the most important. They raise your energy level. Get all of these you can since you have to pause the action to see your life meter.

Force Shields—each one has a red dot on it. They make you invulnerable for a short time.

Smart Bombs—they destroy all of the enemies on screen.

Stasis Bombs—freeze all enemies for a short time.

Magnets—stay away from these! They freeze you for a short time.

Security Keys—get all of these you can. These are the only way to get through doors that block your way.

Computer Disks—you need all of them to get to the lair of Magneto for the final battle.

The mission on the top of the list takes place in Future City. Once beautiful, this city has been ravaged by Magneto and clan. The town is full of mutant creatures and robot tanks.

You may want to use Iceman in this level because of his speed and ability to blast enemies with his beams. Storm does well here too.

In this level you encounter lots of robot tanks and magnetic mutant worms. None of them is particularly dangerous by itself. The real challenge here is that so many come at you at once.

As you work your way up through the streets of the city, you come to a blue door that opens and closes. Time your crossing very carefully, or fight until you get a Force Shield power-up. Either of these techniques works with most of the obstacles you come to.

When you get to the top of the street, you'll see a blue portal in the upper-right corner. Walk onto it and you materialize in another location. There's another portal in the lower left corner of the room. Go for it.

Keep working your way up and down the screens and use the portals to get through the maze.

You will come to a screen with two portals and a single wide gash in the pavement. Lots of robot worms will appear from the gash. Stand to the left of the gash and blast worms as they appear—you'll get a lot of points.

Watch out for the odd-colored tiles on the floor. They may be energy-robbing booby traps.

Soon you will reach the portal that lies directly under a red and yellow wall. If you go in there without the keys, you'll come to a dead end. Go past the wall to find the keys, then come back.

The rooms where the keys are hidden look like dead ends—they are. Once you get the key by blasting an enemy, leave.

Get both keys and go back to the portal by the red and yellow wall. This is the way to the end of the level. The yellow doors won't open unless you have the keys.

The boss in this level is Boomerang. His name describes his weapons. Blast him to get by and retrieve the computer disk.

Master Tips

❏ If you don't like having two heroes floating around the screen, choose a fighter you like and a weaker fighter like NightCrawler for the computer to control. Don't do anything to help him and he will be killed off quickly. Then you can travel alone without having to wait for him to catch up.

❏ Wolverine and Colossus are good choices for the Subterranean level.

❏ Cyclops and Iceman are well suited for the Search and Destroy mission because they can fight from a distance. Watch out for the blue Instant Death Traps in the floor of this level.

❏ You can actually run around the bosses in the levels to get to the end of the level and still collect the computer disk. But where is Magneto?

Xexyz

Manufacturer: *Hudson Soft*

Up Front

In preparing this section, we had only the pre-production game cartridge for Xexyz. We were so early in the production cycle that we couldn't even get an instruction booklet. Frankly, none of our testers could figure out what the plot of this game was supposed to be, but they had a whale of a time trying to figure it out.

Despite the lack of information available, all of our testers liked this game, so here is everything we know about the game.

The hero's name is Apollo, and he's on a quest to free the Island Queens from the evil wizards that rule the islands. Each Island features different types of terrain and a host of nasties that are trying to keep you from completing your quest.

As you move through the islands, you will find many doorways that you should investigate. Inside, you will find treasures, spells, information, weapon power-ups and mini-bosses.

Getting Started

The action is fairly simple to control:

⬍◀▶	Move around.
▼	Crouch down low.
▲	Aims your weapon straight up.
Ⓐ	Jump.
Ⓐ▲	Jump higher than normal.
Ⓑ	Shoot!

The top of the screen shows your score, force stars, life meter, the current weapon, and how much money you have. The game begins on the Island of Ruins. Begin moving to the right, visiting every doorway you come to.

As you defeat enemies they will drop power-ups that look like small shields. E is money. Small ones are worth one, larger ones are worth five. Shields with an L printed on them will restore your life meter.

One of the first places you will visit is a Treasure Room. Treasure chests are suspended over your head, and a ghost flies back and forth across the screen. Choose a chest and position Apollo under it, then jump up to hit the ghost with your head. The ghost will bounce up and knock down the selected chest to reveal what's hidden inside. You can visit this room twice.

Soon you come to a place where you will find an L power-up sitting next to two blocks. Blast all around that area to reveal a hidden door—you'll have a devil of a time fighting the guy on the other side.

To defeat this guy, time your jumps between his blasts of fire to get close to him. Jump up on top of him and get behind him, firing at the back of his head. Once you're behind him, he can't hurt you.

Moving On

At the far right of this level is a door that will take you into the Mechanic Castle. After you clear all of the power-ups out of the room, jump up into the air vent in the ceiling to continue on your journey. You will find yourself in a small room.

You'll need at least 20 money units to get into the mobile armor suit that is hidden inside the door in the lower-right corner of the room. There is also another air shaft in the ceiling. Check it out before getting into the armor.

Use the mobile armor to float through the next section. You will go down a long corridor from left to right. Along the way will be several power-ups for your weapon. When you get to the end you come to two doors. Take the wrong door and you will have to go through the same corridor again.

Master Tips

❏ When you get to the flying saucer, use it to fly to the boss' room. Your life meter will be completely restored. To beat the boss (a big bug), blast his head while you dodge the fire and flies that he shoots at you.

❏ When you have the ball weapon, use angles and ricochet action to hit enemies in awkward places.

❏ In the rooms where you receive power-ups for your weapon, you should always go out and come back in a second time to get a little extra boost. In level three, this is how you can get the Wave Ball weapon.

❏ Watch out for spider webs—they will stun you for a moment making it easier for enemies to hurt you.

Super Mario Bros. 2

Manufacturer: *Nintendo*

Up Front

If PacMan was the first video game star, Mario is certainly the biggest. This guy has box office appeal! Barbara Walters has been trying to get an interview for years. Mario has appeared in more video games than any other character. He is even the referee in Punch Out. Super Mario Bros. 2 is probably the best selling video game of all time.

One of the reasons for this success is that the Mario series is chock full of surprises, hidden pathways, power-ups, and strange little twists. Players love to trade secrets they have discovered about this game. Being the first to find some new twist to the game can make you the most popular person in school for at least a week.

Getting Started

You begin the game by choosing one of four characters:

Mario	A good all-around character.
Luigi	A real good jumper.
Toad	The strongest and the quickest character.
Princess	She is slow, but she can jump and hang in the air better than Michael Jordan!

You can also change characters between levels unless you get there by warping. To move your character, use the following controls:

◀▶   Move from side to side.

▼   Duck!

▲   Climb and go through doors.

Ⓐ   Jump.

Ⓑ   Pick up objects. Pressing B while holding an object throws it.

The only weapons you get in this game are the ones you pick up. To defeat most enemies you must jump on them or throw something at them.

Each level is timed, so you must get through the level in time. There is, however, plenty of time. Once you know a level pretty well, hang back and look for secrets. Jump into strange places, throw objects in different places. Carry objects into the next screen before throwing them. The folks who wrote this game are playing hide and seek with your mind!

Moving On

When the game begins you are falling onto a ledge. The first enemy you meet is called Shy Guy. You can either pick him up and throw him, or you can jump on him to send him over the edge.

When you jump down to the next ledge, you'll find another Shy Guy. Get rid of him and try pulling up some of the plants and vegetables. You can use these to throw at other enemies. You may need these plants later.

Get to the bottom of the level and go through the red door on the right. Once through the door, move to the right and climb the vine. The first vegetable you come to is a potion. When you throw the potion, a door appears where the bottle lands. When you go through the door, you are temporarily in a sub-world. You will see a mushroom. Pick it up. This gives your life meter an extra block, restoring it.

When you pick up veggies in the sub-world, they turn into coins. At the end of the level, you will be able to use those coins in a slot machine game. Each time you get a match or a cherry you will get a 1-up. The more coins you have, the more chances you have to get 1-ups.

Don't pull up veggies in this sub-world—you only get two chances to pull up coins. Save them for later in a place where there are more veggies to be pulled.

You will leave the sub-world when you go back through the door, or when your time runs out.

The POW blocks are bombs that will clear the screen of enemies. The veggie closest to the second POW is a 1-up. At the bottom of this area is your first encounter with bombs. When you pull up a veggie, it's a bomb. Hold onto it for a second or two until it starts to blink, then throw it at enemies. You can also use bombs to clear a path through blocked passageways.

When you begin to move to the top, you will come across an area with lots of veggies. Pull up a plant to get a potion. Go into the sub-world and pick up as many coins as you can. When time expires, move off the screen through the door and come back to do it again.

When you go back in the door, take a running jump across the waterfall to find a shortcut to the boss. You'll find a ladder going down to a door, but it's blocked by stones. Pull up a veggie to get a bomb. Throw the bomb at the bottom of the ladder to blast an opening, then go through the door. Climb up and to the left. Your character will actually leave the screen and go across the top. When you come down, you'll be in front of Birdo.

Birdo spits eggs at you. Jump up on them, pick them up and throw them back at Birdo. Three hits and he's history. You will be off to the bonus round where you can play your coins for 1-ups.

Master Tips

- ❏ When digging through the sand in World Three, move from side to side so that the Shy Guys won't drop onto your head.
- ❏ When you see jars, jump up on them and crouch down. Some hold interesting surprises. Doing this in a sub-world might warp you someplace else.
- ❏ Catch Mouser's bombs and throw them back at him to defeat him.
- ❏ If you see Starman, touch him to become invulnerable for a short time.
- ❏ In World Six you have to fight Birdo again, but this time he doesn't throw eggs. Whack him with three mushroom blocks to defeat him.

Super Mario Bros. 3

Manufacturer: *Nintendo*

Up Front

Mario is back to his former self again (Mario 2 was just a dream after all), and is again jumping up to knock on blocks to reveal coins and mushrooms. All new action in a familiar package with a whole new bunch of enemies! That's what Mario 3 is all about.

Getting Started

In the one-player game you will be Mario. In the two-player game Luigi makes an appearance. Here are some old and new controller tricks:

◀▶	Move Mario or Luigi right and left.
Ⓑ	Hold down the B button when walking and your character will begin to run.
▲	Climb and enter doors. Press button A at the same time and Mario can go up some pipes.
▼	Squat, enter pipes, and slide down slopes.

Ⓐ   Jump, swim, and fly.

Ⓑ   Pick up items. When Mario turns into a
           raccoon, use B to spin around, whacking things
           and enemies with your tail.

Start   Pause the action.

When the game begins, you are shown a map of the
World you're in. There are eight worlds, each having several
sub-worlds. The sub-worlds are shown by blocks on the map.
As you clear each sub-world, the number block will be
replaced with a block marked M. Use the arrow buttons to
move Mario around, choosing which sub-world or feature to
go to, then press A.

In addition to the sub-worlds, the following features are
available:

Spade Panel	This block looks like a card in suit of Spades. When you go here you will play a game where you must line up the pictures for 1-ups.
N-Spade Panel	This game lets you flip cards to match pictures. Make a match and the pictured item is yours. Miss twice and the game is over.
Mini-Fortress and Locked Doors	Defeat the guard of the mini-fortress, you will get a magic ball and the door will unlock. What's in there?
Toad's House	Toad lives in a mushroom. His house is decorated in Early Treasure Chest. This is a good place to get items.
Hammer Brothers	There is one of these guys on every map. Defeat them for special items.

There are many similarities between this game and the
other two Mario games. This one is very much like the original. Jump onto enemies to defeat them. Pick things up and
throw them. Go down pipes to find hidden rooms. It's all here.

Moving On

In the first set of blocks there's a mushroom that makes Mario big.

When you get to the first white block, jump down on the Koopa (turtle). When it goes back into its shell, pick it up and throw it at the first block. This gives you a feather that turns Mario into Raccoon Mario. If your life meter is full, you can float and fly by pressing A repeatedly. Go see what's up in the clouds. Lots of coins and a 1-up? Maybe.

When you have the raccoon tail, use button B to spin. You can break blocks and defeat enemies this way.

Master Tips

❏ Switch blocks turn shiny gold blocks into coins, or turn coins into blocks. You may want to give up coins to be able to climb. You get a 1-up for every 100 coins.

❏ Collecting cards at the end of a world gives you 1-ups.

❏ Blocks with musical notes printed on them give you a springy bounce. Some of these blocks turn pink when you bang them from underneath. This makes them even springier!

❏ Crouch down on white blocks for several seconds to get behind the scenery. You'll find some amazing things this way.

❏ World Three has a treasure room where you can find the frog suit. In later levels the chest on the right is most likely to contain the best item, but not always.

❏ You can reach Warp Zones by blowing the whistle on the map screen.

Kid Icarus

Manufacturer: *Nintendo*

Up Front

Kid Icarus is an action/adventure game for the younger set, although older kids and adults may enjoy it as well. In terms of difficulty, this game is a tweener. It's somewhat less complex than Castlevania II and has more adventure and shoot 'em up action than A Boy and His Blob. It's easier than Zelda, but harder than Duck Tales.

The story is long and involved and is loosely based on Greek and Roman Mythology. Very loosely! Back when the gods and mankind walked the earth together, Palutena and Medusa, goddesses who ruled the light and dark, got into a little spat. The evil Medusa's army has turned Angel Land upside down. Most of Palutena's soldiers have been turned into stone, the three sacred treasures have been stolen, and darkness rules the land.

In despair, Palutena turns to Pit, a young angel, to champion her cause. His mission (you guessed it)—fight impossible odds, slay monsters, and retrieve the sacred treasures in order to defeat Medusa and free the good goddess from the evil one's dungeon. Not original, but good enough to get the game started.

As you reach the end of each level, you turn in your points for power-ups in the form of extra blocks on your life meter.

As you destroy the bad guys, you collect small hearts, half hearts, and full hearts. Hearts are the money of Angel Land. Pit can then stop in shops and buy potions, feathers (to cushion his fall), and other useful items.

To win the battle, Pit must take on the inhabitants of four different levels. Then, and only then, will he get a chance to take on the evil dame herself—Medusa.

Getting Started

From the title screen, press Start. You can then choose to start a new game or enter a password to continue an old game.

Once the game begins, you will see a strength meter and a heart count in the upper left corner of the screen. This information tells you how close to disaster Pit is and how much he can spend in shops to buy weapons and potions that will help him survive. Here are the controls:

◀▶   Move from side to side.

▲   Point your weapon up.

←	Squat and jump down.
Select	Choose your weapon.
Ⓑ	Fire the currently selected weapon.
Ⓐ	Jump.
Start	Pause the game and view a status board.

The status board shows your total score, your score for the current level, what level you are on, Pit's fighting strength (five arrows is max), and what weapons and treasures Pit has. In the fortresses, this display shows the map, but only after you find the map scroll. For the map to be useful, you also need the torch and the pencil. You must get both of these items again for each fortress.

You must conquer three worlds before you can take on Medusa in stage four. They are the Underworld, the Overworld, and the Skyworld. You must beat a different Boss character in each of the three worlds to gain one of the Sacred Treasures.

 As you work your way through each of the levels, you earn points. After you make it through a level, your points are added to your overall total. If you have enough points, you get a power-up that adds an extra block to your life meter—this makes it harder for your enemies to beat you.

As you destroy the Medusa's legions, you get their hearts, making you even stronger.

Be sure to gather all of the mallets that you can get your hands on. When you get to the fortresses, you'll need the mallets to break the Medusa's spell and turn the statues back into Centurions. In the final battle against the Boss, the freed Centurions will come to your aid. If you've freed enough Centurions, they can inflict over half the damage needed to destroy the Boss.

Take your time. Find places where you can just wait for the enemies to come to you and maximize the number of hearts you earn in each level. This will also increase the number of points you will earn, entitling you to power-ups.

One unusual feature of this game is the way the screens are laid out. In levels 1 and 3, you must climb as you battle the enemies. Very often you can go off the screen to one side and reappear on the other side. Sometimes this is the only way to continue going up. It'll take you a while to get used to it, but you'll manage.

Watch out for the Grim Reaper. If he sees you, he'll call the Reapettes. The Reapettes aren't the girl singers in some rock band—they're a group of flying nasties that are a real pain in the neck. You may be able to sneak up on the Grim Reaper and destroy him without him even noticing.

Along the way, you come across several doorways. Some are shops where you can buy valuable goods, others are Black Markets whose prices are always high.

You can also pick up weapons and hearts in other types of rooms. There are training rooms where you can survive a test to determine whether a god will let you pick a new weapon.

You'll encounter treasure rooms where you must break open urns to see if treasures are inside. Watch out, though; the god of Poverty is hiding in one of the urns. If you choose his urn, you walk out with nothing. After breaking all of the urns you want to break, start collecting. When you touch the first item, all of the unbroken urns disappear. Get the stuff, then get out!

Other rooms are filled with enemies. You can't get out till you wipe them out. This is a great way to get hearts.

You'll also come across rooms that include Sacred Chambers, where friendly gods give you arrows to increase the effectiveness of your weapons. Another room has a hot spring that gives you a complete recharge.

Keep up your strength as much as possible to keep all of your weapons working. These weapons include fire to make Pit's arrows stronger and more accurate, the Sacred Bow which makes arrows fly faster and farther, and the protective crystal—two crystals that circle Pit (except in the Fortresses) as he does battle. Crystals are great—they'll destroy enemies without your help.

Along the way, you may find or buy any of the following items to increase your power and effectiveness:

Mallets—you'll need these to free the Centurions in the fortresses. Each Centurion needs a mallet.

Chalice—This item refreshes one block of your endurance meter with the Water of Life.

Bottle—Bottles contain the Water of Life. When your endurance meter reaches zero, this item refreshes one block, keeping you alive.

Barrel—Without the barrel, you can carry only one bottle of water. The barrel lets you carry eight.

Angel Feathers—If Pit takes a tumble from a high place, the feather will save his life by giving him a soft landing.

Check Sheet—In the fortresses, you'll come across this object that looks like a scroll. It provides you with a map of the fortress.

Torch—This object shows which room you're in when you look at the map.

Pencil—This colors the rooms that you've already visited in the fortress, so you know where you've been.

Credit Card—This lets you buy items you need on credit from black marketers. You can't buy anything else on credit until you've paid back the first loan. Like real credit cards, this can be an expensive way to go.

Moving On

You begin your adventure climbing up from the dungeons of the Underworld. You'll pass two checkpoints (at the end of sublevels), where you can turn in your points and receive power-ups.

Watch out for the McGoo, a hot lava creature that just loves to pop out of the floor and burn Pit.

In level 1-2, some of the floors are icy. Make sure Pit doesn't slide off and get hurt. Jam the controller in the opposite direction of Pit's slide to put on the brakes. You can jump up through the ice from the underside!

Later in level 1, you have to watch out for the pink lava water and the plant tentacles. Neither will do you any good.

In level 1-3 you'll find a harp. Touch it and all the enemies on screen turn to mallets. Quick, grab them—this is a limited-time offer.

Near the end of 1-3 is the first of the training rooms. Make sure you have plenty of endurance on your meter when you get here. The trainer will give you the opportunity to test yourself and claim the weapon of your choice. Win the test, and you get a weapon. Lose, and you may die.

Make sure you have plenty of mallets when you go into the fortress in level 1-4. You can buy more from one of the local vendors, but they're a lot cheaper to earn along the way. Hit as many statues as you can with mallets. You'll need all the friends you can get.

All the fortresses are grids of eight rooms by eight rooms. If you letter the rooms across the top row and number the rooms down the side, you will understand when somebody says, "The Water of Life can be found in A6."

The Boss of level one is Twinbellows, a two-headed dog that spits fire at Pit. Defeat him and you advance to the Overworld.

In the Overworld, you'll find new and different terrors to deal with. One of these is Rokman that falls from the sky. Get under them and shoot—they give up lots of hearts. Just don't let them touch you.

The second door in 2-1 is the Water of Life.

Beware of Micks with big lips. Our tester says they're named after Mick Jagger of the Rolling Stones. Wherever they got their name, steer clear of these guys.

At the beginning of 2-2 you'll see a lion's head against the left wall. If you can jump into it, you might be transported elsewhere. What? And miss all the fun?

In this level you also have to deal with Plutons. Not only are they invulnerable, but if they touch you, they'll steal your weapons! How do you think the Black Marketers get the stuff they sell?

In 2-3 are the floating stones. Some of them will come down on briars. Don't stay on too long.

In the fortresses, watch out for the Eggplant Men. They toss eggplants at you. If one touches you, you turn into an eggplant with legs (not a pretty sight). You can visit stores and get into the Water of Life, but until you visit the Nurse, who heals you, the only way to protect yourself is to run for it.

The Water of Life can be found in A2.

The Boss of this level is called Hewdraw—a snake with a dragon's fire-breathing head. Make sure you have freed lots of Centurions to help you. It dives in arcs over your head. Position yourself to shoot at its nose as it passes close to you.

In level 3, the first door you come to is the Water of Life. Once again you are climbing, fighting as you go.

If you have the Protective Crystal, you can outwit the Grim Reaper. Crouch down so he can't see you, and let the crystals revolving around you do the work on him. For some reason, he can't see the crystals.

In this level, the Plutons have wings! Be on guard or you'll be buying your weapons back from the Black Marketers.

Near the end of level 3, you come across the Grim Reaper. Try to get to the cloud on the left side of the screen. Even though it's on the same level with the Reaper, he can't see you. You can safely blast him from a distance.

The last door in the third level is a store. Make sure you have lots of mallets and bottles of the Water of Life before you go into the Skyworld fortress.

Master Tips

❏ Once you've dispatched Pandora, you have the three treasures and you've earned the Wings of Pegasus. You can actually fly right up to the Medusa and introduce yourself.

❏ The booklet that comes with the game is not kidding when it says to shoot all of the Zuree creatures. If you don't get them all, you'll keep flying through the same stuff over and over until you do.

❏ Here are some passwords that will let you start at different levels:

C0W0Wp O0i000 M7000D I00849

E0W2iI n0d000 sQ001H J500ep

❏ Kid Icarus has many musical clues to warn you of danger.

❏ When you are in a shop, make sure that controller two is plugged in. Press A and B together—the shopkeepers will usually lower their prices. Some will get mad, though, and raise prices.

Mega Man 2

Manufacturer: *Capcom*

Up Front

Well, friends, Dr. Wily is up to his tricks again. He is hatching another plot to conquer the world. Only Mega Man, small in stature but big in heart, can save the world. To put an end to Dr. Wily's plans for world conquest, Mega Man must defeat eight of the nastiest villains who ever worked for a mad scientist.

As Mega Man defeats each of the eight bosses, he collects weapons from them that he can use to continue his quest. Three of the bosses—Air Man, Heat Man, and Flash Man—will also give up special transportation items that Mega Man needs to assault Dr. Wily's Skull Castle.

The game features unlimited continues and passwords that will restore your game for you on another day. The password arrangement is unique in that the password consists not of codes but of dots in a grid. You can also choose either of two skill levels—normal and difficult.

Getting Started

Press Start. The game offers you the choice of skill levels we talked about. Use Select to make your choice, then press Start. The next screen lets you start a new game or enter a password.

The game starts you out at the main screen where you can choose which of the bosses you want to tackle first. You can take them on in any order you want. The only requirement is that you must defeat all eight in order to get a shot at the Doctor. Of course, some bosses are easier to defeat if you have the proper tools. Use the following controls to move Mega Man:

◀▶   Move side to side. (These buttons even control him when he's falling. If you forget this, you'll be in for a few rude shocks.)

↕	Climb up and down ladders.
Ⓐ	Jump!
Ⓑ	Use your weapons. (Mega Man can shoot and jump at the same time.)
Start	Display the weapons screen.

There are really two weapons screens. Choose Next from one to view the other. Use the up and down arrows to select a weapon or option, and press Start to resume the game.

After you defeat Air Man, Heat Man and Flash Man will give you special tools—the levitation platform, the jet sled, and the elevator. You can use these items to get to some out-of-the-way places.

You have to fight a number of tough and varied creatures. Many of them will give you power-ups and 1-ups. Beware of power-ups just sitting around—the ones you don't have to fight for. Many of them seem to be there just to lure you away from the area where the boss is lurking.

Moving On

Most books and articles about this game suggest that you go after Air Man first. The instruction booklet that comes with the game even gives you step by step instructions on how to take on Air Man and beat him. Our expert, however, suggests that you take on Flash Man first. Defeat him, and you get the Time Stopper.

Flash Man lives in an Ice Palace. The footing is sometimes tricky. Don't move too fast—you'll lose your footing and slide into oblivion. If you start to slide, jam the arrow in the opposite direction to put on the brakes. Make your way down and to the right to find Flash Man.

You'll come across a few strange creatures, including a strange fellow that resembles one of the two-legged Imperial Walkers in the the Star Wars movies. Blast him a couple of times, and a little guy in a red suit will fall out and pick a fight. He always shoots in blasts of three, and he seems to forget to keep his shield up. Either take him on or jump over him and move on. There are times when it just doesn't pay to fight!

Eventually, you come to a white door that opens when you walk up to it. Once inside you must fight Flash Man.

He's going to try to use the Time Stopper on you. This weapon freezes everything on the screen for a short time, including Mega Man (unless he's the one using the weapon). Stay in the left corner until Flash Man jets over to you, then jump over him and hide in the deep trough in the middle of the floor. Until he uses the Time Stopper, jump up and blast at him between his bursts of fire. Get right back down in the lower left corner of the trough—he can't shoot you during the Time Stop if you're lower than he is.

Master Tips

Our Mega Man Master has a few tips that will help you get through the levels. Our Master suggests you take on the bosses in the following order (after Flash Man, of course):

Quick Man

❏ Watch out for laser beams. One touch, and you're reaching for the Continue button. Drop past the first group of lasers and work to the left.

❏ When you get to the bottom, start working right until you get to the Hotheads. Take a look at the terrain behind them—you'll have to go through it in the dark after you defeat the Hotheads.

❏ The next area of lasers is intense, but you have the Time Stopper. Work through the first bunch, then activate the Time Stopper. This gives you the time you need to make it through the really tough part.

❏ Quick man is . . . well, quick! The first thing he will do is jump high into the air at you. Run to the middle of the screen and dodge him and his fire while blasting at him. Defeat him, and you get the Quick Boomerang.

Metal Man

❏ You must fight your way through a mechanized world full of crushers and conveyor belts. Jump to move the opposite way the conveyor belt is moving.

- ❏ One of the creatures you must fight looks like a stack of oil drums. It's only vulnerable around the eyes.
- ❏ To beat Metal Man, stay to the left. Don't let the conveyer belt pull you close to him. Keep blasting while you jump over the buzz saw gears he hurls at you. Defeat him, and his gear weapon is yours.

Air Man

- ❏ Air Man lives in the clouds. For a detailed description on this level, refer to the instruction booklet. It contains four pages of instructions on how to beat this level.
- ❏ Use the Lightning Lord's flying platforms to your advantage.
- ❏ Use the Quick Boomerang to make quick work of Air Man. His weapon sends out patterns of tornadoes. Jump them, and get close for the most effective use of the boomerang.

Bubble Man

- ❏ To beat Bubble Man, dodge the lead bubbles and use the Quick Boomerang. When you defeat him, you get the power to hurl lead bubbles.
- ❏ Once you've defeated all eight bosses, you are equipped to take on the doctor himself. Of course, you will have to fight each of these bosses one more time before you can get to Wily. This time, though, you have all the weaponry in your favor. It will be much easier, or will it?

The Evil Doctor Wily

- ❏ Use the Metal Blade to defeat the blocks that transform into robots.
- ❏ Some floors are not as solid as they seem. Try bowling with lead bubbles when in doubt.
- ❏ When you get into the cave with the red acid dripping from the ceiling, DON'T STOP! Just keep running through the area to avoid being dissolved.
- ❏ Dr. Wily is a sneak. You will have to fight him twice too.
- ❏ Ok, now go back and do it on the difficult setting!

The games in this section are based on military operations ranging from guerrilla warfare to submarine attacks. All of these games feature brave soldiers fighting against impossible odds. Enough hand-to-hand combat and sophisticated weaponry to keep the most experienced soldier of fortune on edge!

Military Games

Contra

Manufacturer: *Konami*

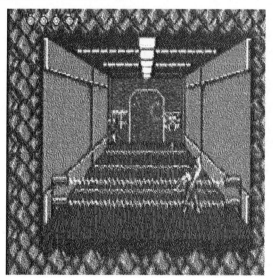

Up Front

Way back in 1957, deep in the Amazon basin, a large hunk of space debris crashed through Earth's atmosphere and landed in the jungle. Because the area was so far from civilization and because nobody knew all that much about the object, few people paid much attention to the event.

What the world didn't know, and the Pentagon has only recently discovered, is that this seemingly trivial event has Earth-shattering potential! The object wasn't just some piece of cosmic trash—it carried the evil Red Falcon and his hideous horde of horrible henchmen. Fearing the political repercussions of an all out assault, the Pentagon Brass have recruited a small band of brave fighters to wipe out the Red Falcon before he can carry out his plan to dominate the world.

Ok, so its not the most original plot in the world, but it does set the stage for one of the fastest paced fighting games ever. You must either single-handedly (or with a buddy) wipe out this army of alien invaders in an all out war, or life as we know it may cease to exist forever!

There are very few niceties about Contra. This is one straightforward, action-packed shoot 'em up. But despite the high level of violence, this game offers many lessons in cooperation. Two players working together have a somewhat easier time making it through the fray.

To make it through to the end, you must fight your way through eight different defensive areas. The eighth and final zone is the lair of the Red Falcon himself.

Getting Started

Getting started in Contra is easy. Simply choose the one-player or two-player mode and start fighting. Use the following controls to fight:

↕ ◀▶	Move around the screen and aim your weapon.
▶	Move right and aim straight right.
▶ →	Move right and aim weapon down.
▶ ↗	Move right and aim weapon up at an angle.
◀ →	Move left and aim weapon down.
◀ ↗	Move left and aim weapon up.

⬆   Aim weapon straight up without moving.

⬇   Lay belly down, facing either left or right
       depending on which way you were facing before
       you hit the dirt.

Ⓑ   Fire your weapon.

Ⓐ   Jump in the direction you're facing.

Don't worry about ammo—you have all you can use and
then some. You start out with just a simple military assault
rifle. As you knock out gun placements, pill box sensors (sensors alert the Red Falcon to your presence), and flying capsules, you can upgrade your weapons. These power-ups last
until your guy gets knocked off. Upgrades include machine
guns, laser fire, fire balls, rapid fire as well as bullet proof
force fields (temporary) and the mass destruction weapon.

You begin with three lives. For every stage you make it
through, you gain an extra life. When you've lost all of your
lives, you can choose Continue up to three times.

Moving On

To get through the opening rounds, you need to be prepared
for action in some special areas. The following sections tell
you what to expect.

Jungle

The action begins along the river bank. You make your way
deeper into the jungle as you move to the right. Beware of the
bridges—they have sensors that begin blowing up the bridge
the moment you set foot on them. Take the bridge route by
jumping. If you fall in the water, keep firing and swimming
until you get to land. As you knock out gun placements and
pill boxes, bird-shaped symbols appear. Pick these up to
upgrade your weapon, jump over them if you like the weapon
you have. You can shoot down flying capsules for weapons
upgrades as well.

At the end of the jungle run, you come to the outside
wall of Base 1. This base is guarded by a sensor and two guns
that shoot fire balls. Knock out the guns and blast the sensor
(several times) to knock a hole in the wall for entry to the
base.

Base 1

Once inside the base you have to fight through the corridors. You'll go through a series of rooms guarded by electric beams. Stay behind the beams and blast away at the guns and sensors in the wall. As if this isn't tough enough, enemy soldiers will come around the corner and blast at you with rifles, grenades, and rolling barrels. Enemies in red uniforms give up weapons upgrades when you hit them.

The last screen is a lulu! By the time you get there, you will have wiped out all the soldiers. It's just you and the wall. Blast those sensors!

Waterfall

Once past Base 1 you have to work your way up the waterfall. Watch out for enemy fire and falling boulders. The guys in the water will be launching three-shot grenades. Jump and dodge, but above all keep firing. At the top of the waterfall is the toughest foe yet! This hideous creature has flailing arms that launch fire balls. First get the arms, then fire into its mouth to get into Base 2.

Base 2

This section of terrain is a lot like Base 1 only tougher. The sensors are harder to knock out because many of them have a protective shield that you must blow away first. It's a good thing you have unlimited ammo.

At the end of Base 2 (if you get this far) is a four-headed monster sitting on the top of a wall. Blast the sensors! The monster's heads move back and forth; when they're aligned one behind the other, blast 'em. This is the only time they're vulnerable.

Snow field

Well it's time to move back outdoors for some more fun and games. By this time, the Red Falcon knows that you're no amateur out for a picnic. The sledding really gets tough here. Not only are there more enemy troops per square kilometer, but unseen nasties are lurking behind the trees tossing concussion grenades at you. You can't blast them and you can't blast the grenades. Jump, boy, jump! Unlike the jungle sequence, you can't take a swim—the icy cold water will freeze you to death, unless of course you go splat on the ice.

Toward the end of this battle you have to cross over some metal pipes. Just when you think you've made it across, you'll find that the Falcon has sent an armored, armed tractor-like vehicle to mow you down. Move to the far left of the screen and blast away while staying away from the fire of its guns. You'll know its about to blow when it starts to glow red.

The end of the snow field brings an airborne ship that keeps sending out death pods after you. If you're playing with a friend, one of you should fight off the pods while the other blasts the sensors on the bottom of the ship. Be careful—this guy disappears and reappears in different places.

Master Tips

❏ There's nothing delicate about Contra. It's a shoot 'em up of the first magnitude. Brute force wins every time.

❏ You can start the game with thirty lives for each player by using the following keys:

➔ ➔ ➔ ➔ ◀▶ ◀▶ Ⓑ Ⓐ Start

This effectively gives you 120 lives, because you can have three continues of thirty lives each.

❏ If you are short of lives and get killed, you can swipe a life from your buddy by pressing button A as your soldier recovers.

Jackal

Manufacturer: *Konami*

Up Front

Alright, so Chuck Norris and Rambo have been to the jungle and brought home some of our POWs that were left behind so many years ago, but they didn't get them all. Dozens of them are still held captive. An all-out invasion is out of the question, so the President has selected a small group of specially trained commandos to take on the job. Your mission—to sneak past the Cambodian border and get them out.

This is an action shoot 'em up in the fine tradition of Contra and Iron Tank. Unlike other Konami games, the secret password to get thirty men doesn't work. With limited continues you're going have to work for every POW you send home. In the two-player mode a friend can help you along, just as in Contra.

Getting Started

This game is the most arcade-like of Konami's war games. The controls are extremely simple and few:

⬍◀▶	Move the jeep around the screen.
Ⓑ	Fire the machine gun.
Ⓐ	Fire the hand grenades. (Hand grenades can be upgraded to different types of bazooka missiles.)

You must clear the POWs out of six enemy territories before your mission is a success. Along the way you will have to battle several different types of tanks, cannons, helicopters, planes, boats, and foot soldiers.

 You will find weapon upgrades in some unlikely spots, and you'll get them from rescued POWs as well. You begin with hand grenades. Your first power-up will be to bazooka missiles. The second power-up extends the power of the projectiles, adding two after-blasts to the sides of the impact. The third power-up changes the two-way blast into a four-way blast. If you get knocked off (and you will), your jeep is armed only with hand grenades and a machine gun until you get powered up again.

You don't have energy meters or anything like that in this game. Take a hit and you're history. Nobody said it would be easy.

Moving On

Your infiltration squad is airlifted into the border area along the coast. Move to the northeast and blast the first green hut you come to. This hut contains the bazooka power-up. You'll be blasting many similar huts to free prisoners before long.

Throughout the game your basic heading will be to the North. As you move north from the hut, you'll come across two 50-mm cannons. Approach slowly and see what their range is, how fast their shots travel, and how they react to your movements. Notice that their shots are white. Later you will see cannons that shoot yellow projectiles which travel much farther. Once you've taken out the cannons, blast a hole in the gate and start rescuing the prisoners held in the huts. Don't get hit now! You will lose some of the POWs. 1-ups are based on points and POWs rescued.

Head west over the bridge and take a right to head north again. You will be near water. Whenever you're near water, watch out for gun boats and submarines. You can't outrun heat-seeking missiles—you must shoot them down.

There's one more POW hut before you get to the helipad to transfer them to the chopper. Pull up in the area marked STOP. Once the POWs are safely on the chopper, head north again to fight the four blue tanks. Hit them once, they turn red; hit them again, they explode.

On to Checkpoint Baker, as lovely a level as ever tried to waste you. Right at the start of the maze you'll find prisoners to rescue. Avoid the cannon fire and get them. Next comes an aerial attack. Dodge the bombs or shoot them before they hit.

When you get to the water, blast the statue before he spits heat seekers at you. You have now had a preview of the end of this level.

When you come to the columns on the left side, go in and put a blast on the lower left corner. There's a power-up hidden there.

Move north and take out the missile-spitting heads to move on to the next level. These missiles are heat seekers, and you can't outrun them. As they come in on you, shoot 'em down.

Master Tips

❏ When you see the white helicopter fly over you heading north, you're nearing the end of the level. Look for a helipad.

❏ Although you can't shoot bazooka missiles through a wall, you can destroy enemies on the other side in complete safety. If you have the two-way or four-way shot power-up, the after-blast will travel over the wall and get whatever's there. If you're using the two-way blast, make sure your enemy is to your right or left.

❏ In early levels arrows painted on the roadway usually point the right direction. In later levels, though, they may be traps leading you into dead ends.

❏ You'll see cannons on the gun boat at the end of the third level. Wait till the hatches are open to fire—this is the only time you can inflict damage.

❏ Try to stay on dry land in the fourth level. The wet parts will slow you down and make maneuvering difficult.

Metal Gear

Manufacturer: *Konami*

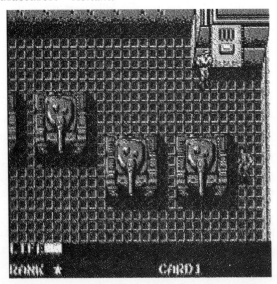

Up Front

Metal Gear is a hard game to describe. At first it seems like just another war time shoot 'em up with loads of senseless violence. The further you get into Metal Gear, though, the more

Double Dragon II (Acclaim)

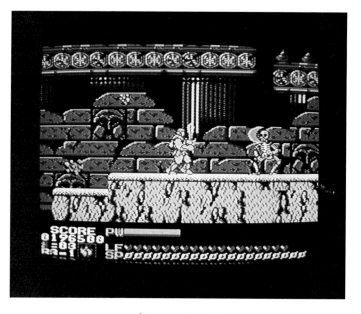

Astyanax (Jaleco)

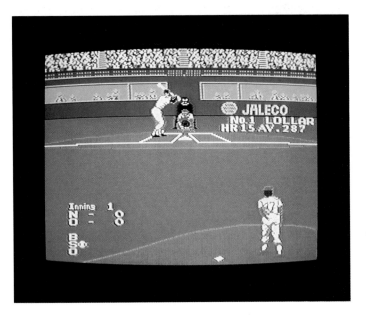

Bases Loaded II (Jaleco)

Sesame Street 123 (High Tech)

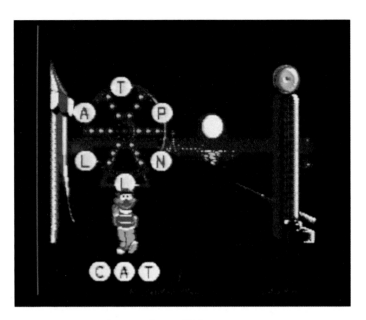

Sesame Street ABC (High Tech)

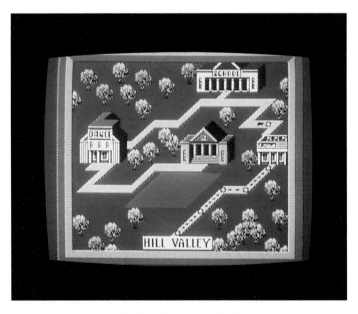

Back to the Future (LJN)

Who Framed Roger Rabbit? (LJN)

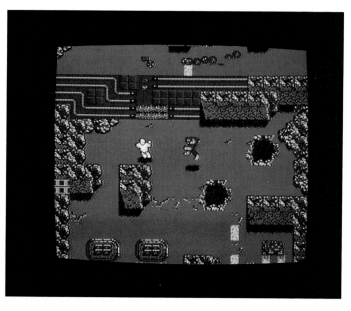

The Uncanny X-men (LJN)

Stealth ATF (Activision-Mediagenic)

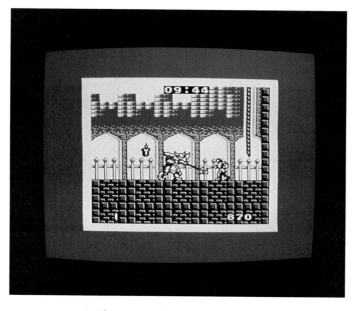

Castlevania II: Simon's Quest (Konami)

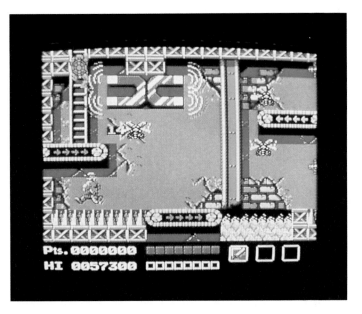

Teenage Mutant Ninja Turtles (Ultra Software)

Metal Gear (Konami)

Silent Service (Konami)

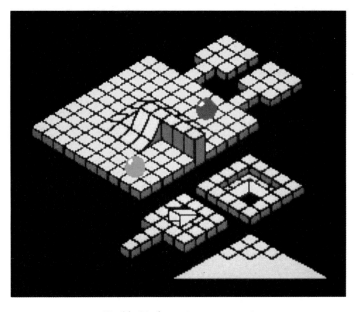

Marble Madness (Milton Bradley)

Super Dodge Ball (CSG Imagesoft)

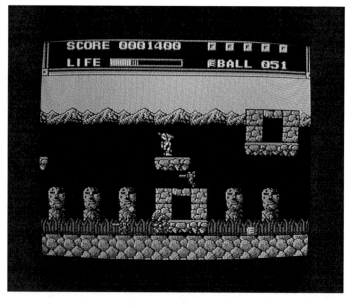

Xexyz (Hudson Soft)

you realize that this game has some substance to it. You'll have to pardon the comparison—Metal Gear is a bit like Zelda with hand grenades.

The story is predictable. Colonel Vermon CaTaffy (some newspapers spell it Vermin QuaTaffy) grew up in Outer Mongolia tending the family sheep herd and looking after his 27 sisters. As we all know, the pressures of this kind of a life can turn even the best boy bad, and so Colonel CaTaffy has taken to a life of international terrorism. His base of operations is a small country near South Africa called Outer Heaven. CaTaffy and his boys are building the ultimate weapon for ruling the world, Metal Gear.

You are Solid Snake, the hero of Grenada. You have brains, brawn, and the bravery needed to carry out an attack with speed and agility.

CaTaffy has five buildings from where he launches his dirty work. Your mission is to infiltrate all of his strongholds, release hostages, and destroy Metal Gear.

Getting Started

It takes a while to get going in this game. You won't beat it in a day or two, so there's a password provision that lets you pick up where you left off. From the opening screen you should choose either Start, which will begin a new game, or Password, which will let you resume a previous contest. Then use the following controls for your maneuvers:

⬍◀▶	Move up, down, left and right.
Ⓑ	Deliver deadly punches.
Ⓐ	Fire your currently selected weapon.
Start	Pause.
Select	Select weapons and equipment, and communicate.

On the bottom of the screen is a status bar that shows you a Life Graph, your rank, and which weapons and equipment you've selected. When the Life Graph hits zero, you're done for. Your rank begins with one star. As you free hostages you get promoted (five stars is the highest rank). With each promotion you can carry more ammo and supplies.

At various times during the game, you will see the word CALL flash in the status area. This means that Big Boss or one of the other people in your organization is trying to reach you. Most of the time they have some bit of important information for you.

You begin your mission with just your fists and a pack of cigarettes. To acquire weapons you must find them in trucks and in the buildings that you must infiltrate.

Moving On

The map that comes with the game shows most of the things you'll need in the early stages. But even with the map, this game's not easy. If you're renting the game or you've lost the map, you should make your own on a piece of graph paper.

You begin in the jungle outside the Colonel's fortress. Move to the right and wait for the guy by the jeep to fall asleep, but don't wait too long or he will wake up and come after you. In the next two screens, you must run through the guard dogs. If you get trapped, use your fists. You will come upon a trail where two soldiers are standing guard. Sneak up on them as they have their backs turned.

You will find that most of the enemy soldiers are pretty dumb. You can usually sneak right up behind them when they're looking the other way. When there are two or more soldiers in the same screen, you have to knock them off one by one without alerting the others. If they spot you, you can either fight or run out of the room. The soldiers won't follow you from room to room. Apparently they don't have a great communications system. As our tester so aptly put it, "No wonder this guy (CaTaffy) is losing the war—he hires the wrong people."

In the screen below the guard shack, make sure you look in all the trucks from top to bottom. The bottom truck will begin to move when you step in. This is your ride to Building 1.

By the time you get into Building 1, you will have several pieces of equipment, and Card 1. In the trucks outside of Building 1 you'll find rations for recharging your life meter. You can get up to three rations for each star of rank you have.

Enter the building and start looking for weapons and hostages. You'll find weapons in one place and the ammunition you need in another. The amount of ammo you can carry depends on your rank. As you run out of ammo you'll need to go back to those same spots where you found ammo for resupply.

Be sure to look in all the trucks, but be careful—some trucks contain soldiers. Be ready at all times.

To find one particular hostage in Building 1, you'll need to be captured. Step into the truck in the room at the bottom right of the maze—it's the only truck in the room. Of course you lose all of your weapons and ammo, but they're not all that hard to get back. Go into the room where the Shot Gunner stands guard, and run immediately to the door at the bottom right of the screen. There you will find your weapons.

Master Tips

❏ Keep an eye out for laser cameras. Stay in the shadows where they can't detect you. In the early going, they sound an alert. In later stages, they'll shoot at you as well.

❏ Yellow puffs of smoke signal poison gas. Get your gas mask on, quick!

❏ If a door doesn't open, try a different key card. If the room contains ammo and it isn't a full supply, go out and come back in until you have all you can hold.

❏ The missile is a very important weapon because you can guide it around corners. Use it to knock out the control panel to de-electrify the floor in those rooms where the floor glows. You can run through real fast while eating rations if you have to, but you might not make it and you surely won't have any rations left for later.

❏ Don't accidentally shoot a hostage! You lose a star if you do!

❏ Have you noticed that you always get warnings of poison gas and the like just a little too late? Or that Big Boss seems to misdirect you at times? Is there something sinister about this?

❏ Here is a head start password that will give you just about everything that you can get in Building 1 without Card 4:

35ZQE IBZ3A 56645 F14C6 NS1K6

Now get back in there, see what you were doing wrong, and then start over.

Silent Service

Manufacturer: *Konami*

Up Front

Silent Service is one of the most complex games ever to come to the Nintendo system. In this World War II simulation, you take command of an American submarine in the Pacific theatre. From your bases at Midway, Fremantle, and Brisbane, you take off looking for Japanese shipping vessels and troop carriers, in an attempt to disrupt their operations.

The concept behind this game is to re-create the conditions under which the submariners of the Pacific fought in "The Big One" nearly fifty years ago. This simulation offers detail to spare, and to be successful, you'll have to pay attention to every one of them.

There is no one way of playing this game. There are so many variables and so many potential winning (and losing) strategies, it's nearly impossible to outline a winning strategy for you. The best we can do is introduce you to your ship and send you out on some practice runs with a few hints.

Getting Started

You have your choice of three different modes of play: torpedo/ gun practice, convoy action, and war patrol.

Torpedo/gun practice lets you get used to the controls for the sub. Four old hulks are anchored off the base island. You get to try anything you want in relative safety—they won't fire at you. About all you can do to mess up is to ram one of them.

Convoy action takes you into specific battles. Six different scenarios are available ranging from a day time surface attack to a blind nighttime radar mission. Each convoy is different and requires a different strategy.

War patrols take you into the Pacific on extended cruises. You either get back to base or you don't. If you're sunk, or if you run out of fuel, you can't return to base. This is the most difficult part of the game to master. The strategy involves using all of your resources to achieve the maximum results.

As you leave the base, use the arrow keys to steer your sub into the shipping lanes. The screen shifts from light blue to dark blue to show you the passing of day and night. When enemy vessels are spotted, the screen turns red. Press A to engage them.

Once you've chosen your mission, a menu appears that lets you change settings to affect the skill level. You can set the following items:

Limited	When you choose limited
	visibility, Visibility ships that
	are out of radar range do not
	appear on the map. Unlimited
	visibility makes all enemy
	ships visible for as far away
	as the map extends.
Convoy	One of the defensive
Zig Zags	measures taken by convoys in
	WWII was to cut an irregular
	path across the sea in hopes
	of making it harder to hit
	them with torpedoes. If you
	turn off the zig zag, it makes
	convoys steam ahead in a
	line.
Dud Torpedoes	When you have a torpedo
	that just goes clank against
	the hull of an enemy ship,
	you have a problem,
	especially since it takes a
	couple of minutes to reload
	the tubes. Submariners on

	both sides had this problem on occasion. If you choose no Dud Torpedoes, all of your shots that hit the target will explode.
Port Repairs Only	You can either choose to let damage to your sub be repaired at sea, or you can choose port repairs as a handicap.
Expert Destroyers	When you choose Expert Destroyers, the captain and crew (especially the sonar operator) are better trained and more skilled than average.
Convoy Search	Convoy Search adds a touch of realism to your game. You have to look for convoys to attack. The opposite choice, Close Convoys, makes finding the enemy a lot easier— they're usually in the immediate area.

The controls for this game are very simple. Use the arrow buttons to move a yellow arrow around the screen to point at whatever you want to control or activate, then press button A.

Moving On

Once you put out to sea, all of the action is centered around the conning tower where the periscope is located. All of the other action in the game is accessed from this point. To see the conning tower view at any time, press Select.

As you move the arrow around the screen, the Captain will move from station to station. To view a station, move the Captain there and press A.

At the bottom of the screen is a *console* that lets you control your ship. Each time you access a control, you will receive a message at the top of the console. To change a control, point at it and press A. Various symbols from left to right stand for the following controls:

Engines	This control has five settings (0-4) that range from full stop to flanking speed. The R in a box stands for reverse.
Direction Control	This is the box with four arrows around it. The up arrow surfaces the sub, down arrow dives. The left and right arrows control the rudder for turning. When you point to one of the arrows and press A, the arrow stays lit. You must point to the box and press A to cancel the arrow. For example, if you choose the right arrow, the sub moves around in a circle until you choose the box to return the rudder to its middle position.
The Chart	This symbol shows two maps, one large one small. By choosing one or the other, you can zoom into and out of the view of your location. If you are close enough, you will actually be able to see enemy vessels on the map.
Periscope	Choose the periscope symbol to raise and lower the periscope.
The Clock	On the right side of the console is a clock with the marks F and N. This lets you speed up and slow down time. You can use the clock to condense an hour's chase into a couple of minutes. You can set time scales from normal to eight times normal.

In any station on the conning tower except the naviga-tion table, the map is replaced by the symbols for the deck gun and the torpedoes. To fire the deck gun and torpedoes, point to the symbols and press A. Remember that you have limited ammunition and that it takes a few minutes to load the torpedoes into the tubes. If you fire all torpedoes at once, you have to wait until the crew reloads before you can fire again.

The deck gun is only available when you are on the surface. You can aim the deck gun by using the number two controller's up and down arrows. This puts more or less arc on your shot, making the shot go long or short.

There are torpedoes both fore and aft. If you're out of forward torpedoes, shoot from the hip . . . I mean the stern.

Master Tips

❏ Remember that submarines are offensive weapons. It takes daring and resourcefulness to stay alive at sea for weeks at a time. Don't do anything rash. Try to sneak up on the convoys and make your first torpedoes count.

❏ Some convoys are sitting ducks, and others are heavily protected by destroyers that will come after you as soon as you make a move or get too close. You can try to out-run them, turn and fight them head on, or dive and run silent.

❏ One way of fooling destroyers is to release oil and debris to make them think you've been sunk. Press A and B on controller both at the same time to try this maneuver. You can only pull this one once per mission, however.

❏ A very risky, but fun, attack is to submerge and wait for a convoy to come into range. Surface quickly and blast away.

❏ You must be sure of the terms Heading and Bearing. The heading is the direction the sub is traveling. The Bearing is the direction you are looking through the periscope or binoculars. Both Heading and Bearing are measured in degrees. Zero degrees is North, 180 is South.

Stealth ATF

Manufacturer: *Activision*

Up Front

This arcade style game puts you in the cockpit of the Stealth ATF, one of the world's most advanced fighter planes. Take to the skies in over a hundred missions of real shoot 'em up action.

This game is as straightforward as they come. You must complete over a hundred missions of dogfighting to beat this game. Each mission builds on the last. No tricks or surprises. As you progress through the missions, they get harder and faster, with more enemy planes trying to blast you out of the sky.

Getting Started

To begin the game, choose the one-player or two-player mode. In the two-player mode, you and a friend take turns flying missions. But you don't have to choose the two-player mode to use a second player. The second player can take the other controller and give the enemy pilots a hand. Now the bogey (enemy plane) closest to the center of the screen is under the command of the second player, who can cause you all sorts of new problems.

Each mission consists of three stages—take-off, fighting, and landing. Taking off and landing are simple to do, although there's always a chance that you'll mess up and make a big hole in the ground.

To take off from the air base, hold down the A button to gain speed. The speed meter is in the status bar at the bottom of the screen. When the dot goes around the right side of the meter and wraps back to the left, press the down arrow to lift the nose of the plane. Off you go!

When you're airborne, use the following controls to move your airplane and fight:

⬍	Bank and turn.
⬍	Climb and dive.
Ⓐ	Fire the cannon!
Ⓑ	Launch you missiles.
Start	Stealth mode. Enemy radar has trouble finding you. You have a better chance of sneaking up on them.
Select	Pause game. Select also turns off the music and sound.

Read-outs on the cockpit panels tell you how many bogeys you have shot down, how many missiles remain, your altitude, and so on. The radar in the middle of the panel shows you where bogeys are.

After the mission, hold down button B until you lose air speed. The plane practically lands itself. Most new players try to keep the nose up and do other things to land, which is why they crash so often.

Moving On

Your first mission is simple. Go after four bogeys and shoot them down. You start out with eight missiles. Don't waste them or you'll be left with only cannon fire.

As you fly along, watch the radar screen to see where bogeys are. Line them up in the center of your screen as close to the cross hairs as possible. If they are just the right distance away from you, they'll be framed by your radar. This frame and the beeping noise tell you that you have missile lock on them. Press B to fire the missile. Don't wait too long or they'll fly right by the missile and go past you.

When an enemy plane goes by you, go nose up and over to give chase.

Master Tips

❏ We can't give you a lot of advanced information about this game. As you progress through the missions, you'll see different locations and times of day. The number, speed, and aggressiveness of the enemy will change as well.

❏ This game does not offer continues, not even secret ones. Hit the silk three times and you're out of the game.

❏ You earn bonus rounds when you handle a mission well. In the bonus round, bogeys don't attack. You can rack up big extra point counts downing these planes before time runs out.

❏ Your instrument panel warns you when incoming missiles are attacking. Duck and dodge. Watch out for bogeys that have gone past you—they may double back to get you. Remember, they get more and more aggressive as the missions go on.

Top Gun II

Manufacturer: *Konami*

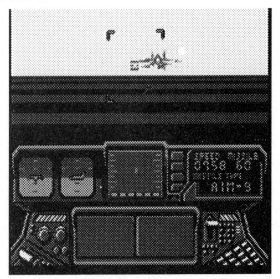

Up Front

The earliest fighter pilots used pistols and hand grenades to bring down enemy planes. Later, machine guns, jet engines, advanced electronics, and air-to-air missiles would elevate the deadly art of dogfighting to the peak of technology.

All of this advanced technology is housed in the F-14 Tomcat. And here's your chance to climb into the cockpit to see whether or not you have the right stuff.

Top Gun II offers three different styles of play. If dog-fighting is your style, choose either the one-player vs. the Game mode, or the two-player dogfight. For hot and heavy shoot 'em up or be-shot action, choose the one-player mission game.

Getting Started

The one-player modes require two skills—not only do you have to be able to fly and fight, you must also be able to land on a carrier. You may have just downed an entire squadron of enemy planes without a scratch, but if you can't put that baby down on a flattop you're history. Use the following controls to fly and land:

Flying

◀▶	Bank and turn. Tap either one twice to do a barrel roll (a good way to avoid missiles).
▲▼	Control the flaps to gain or lose altitude. This depends on the mode you choose from the opening menu. You can select normal or reverse stick.
▲▼	Tap either one twice to do a loop.
Ⓐ	Increase your speed.
Ⓑ	Fire the cannon. Tap B twice to launch missiles when the red missile lock arrow is showing.

Landing

▲▼◀▶	Move in the direction called for on the radar display.
Ⓐ	Increase speed.
Ⓑ	Put on the air brakes.

Before the mission starts, you can choose any of three different types of missiles. Each missile has a different size frame for missile lock (the ability to launch). The larger the number of missiles, the smaller the lock frame. To get a missile lock, you must get the bogey in your sights inside the lock frame.

The two-player game is the best place to learn how to fly the aircraft without getting shot at. Even if you're by yourself, choose this mode. The other fighter will just fly along at about the same speed as you. Practice flying maneuvers. See how the other plane looks on your radar and how its radar position changes as you fly around.

Bring yourself around in back of the other plane and see what a missile lock looks like and what getting hit with a few cannon shots looks like from inside the other guy's canopy. Oh what the heck, give him a Sidewinder right up the old exhaust nozzle, it's only a multi-million dollar airplane, and the pilot has a parachute.

Notice that there is no altimeter. You don't have to worry about hitting the deck. You only have a limited number of missiles, but you have all the cannon fire a jet jock could want.

Once you're comfortable with the controls of the plane, try the one-player game.

Moving On

In the one-player game you perform a series of three missions beginning with a real tough overseas adventure.

Just sit tight as you and your plane are brought up on the elevator. You will hear the engines rev up and you'll be launched. As soon as the nose levels out on the artificial horizon display, you have control over the airplane.

Get settled in quickly—the enemy's not going to give you much time. If the constant barrage of enemy fighters isn't enough, you'll also have to cope with deadly submarines and destroyers. Knock down the cruise missile, and you'll get to see if you can land this thing.

The second mission takes you over land targets in search of the Hind-Alpha helicopter. And you thought the first mission was tough! The third mission takes you to the edge of space as you take on a Star Wars combination of deadly laser beams and a hot rod, armed-to-the-teeth space shuttle.

So you think you are some kind of pilot, right? Then try the one-player vs. the game mode. In this variation of the game, you take on a succession of Russian aces in one-on-one dogfights. Each one is a better pilot than the last. If you make it through these seven opponents, you can really call yourself a Top Gun.

Master Tips

❑ Barrel rolls and evasive maneuvers are your best defense against bogeys closing in on you.

❑ You'll see several alert lamps on the right side of your control panel. The top one lights when you're in danger. The second one lights when a bogey gets a missile lock on you. When that second light comes on, you had better be jigging and spinning like a kid with a worm down his back or you're toast.

❏ When you're in a steep turn, you'll notice that your cannon fire is pushed off to one side by the slipstream of air moving past the nose of your plane. Keep this in mind when a bogey comes into your sights because your bullets aren't hitting the center of the cross hairs anymore.

❏ The same is true of missiles. A missile launched in passing has much less chance of hitting home than a missile that's launched straight at the target. Learn to lead your shots for a better chance of hitting the bogey.

Iron Tank

Manufacturer: *SNK*

Up Front

1944. London sits in cinders. Winston Churchill rallies the valiant Brits into a fighting force second only to the Americans. Edward R. Murrow reports to the folks at home about the current situation. And Eisenhower is planning the Normandy Invasion. Before the big assault, someone's got to knock out the enemy's long-range cannon. Paul, code named Iron Snake, is chosen for his skill and bravery.

Armed with only a map and a ten-ton tank, Paul must take on the Hun single-handedly . . . and win.

This game is interesting in that it lets you take any of several different routes and make your final assault from any of three roads. Some of the ways are harder than the others —it's like having three games in one. The game also offers unlimited continues and a password feature that lets you pick up where you left off.

Getting Started

You begin with a tank and a not-so-powerful weapons system. Along the way, you collect power-ups that provide you with the added strength you need. Use the following controls to move your tank:

⬍◀▶	Move your tank around the screen.
Ⓑ◀▶	Press B while holding down the left or right arrow to turn the gun turret.
Ⓐ	Fire the turret-mounted cannon.
Ⓑ	Fire the machine gun.

Press Select to see the map and the condition of your power-ups. At this menu, you can also decide which of your power-ups you want hooked into the cannon. Several different types of power-ups are available. They appear on the ground as red shapes marked by letters.

E—energy. When your energy runs out, so do you. You can store energy in a spare tank and use it to refill your main tank.

B—explosive power. It increases the power of your cannon.

L—long-range additive. This power-up will increase the distance your cannon shoots.

F—armor piercing capability. This is quite useful in dealing with some of the super tanks you come across.

?—the secret weapon. It might be the enemy's new bomb. Keep it in reserve for the really tough times ahead.

As you move through the highways and byways of wartime France, keep in touch with your unit. Use the radio. When you're receiving a call, you'll see a message flashing on the screen and hear a beeping noise. Take the call—you'll learn some important information. You can learn other important information from the POWs that you find and free along the way.

You will be attacked by tanks and infantry soldiers, planes and trains, not to mention the Big Bertha Blaster Bombs that fall from the sky.

Whenever you can, run over your enemies rather than shoot them. Infantry grunts add a lot to your energy reading.

Moving On

Hit the beach! After landing, head Northeast, toward the fork in the road. Enemy foot soldiers and tanks come swarming down on you. Keep an eye out for power-ups, and run over as many enemies as you can. When you see the big bomb coming down from above, keep to the left of the path, as far from the blast as you can. If you're far enough away, the bombs can't hurt you.

Fight your way to the fork in the road. Take the right fork to avoid the long bridges—it's difficult to see what's going on as you look down through the steel beams over the top of the bridges.

You can mix and match your power-ups on the cannon. Don't use up your long-range ability when you're fighting up close. Power-ups have limited capacity. Don't use them up if you don't have to.

Soon you'll come to the first enemy base. Stay to the bottom of the screen and you'll be out of range of the cannon fire from the wall. Inch up and blast each cannon twice to destroy them. Once you silence the cannon fire, you have to defeat several tanks before you can get inside the base. Make your way through. Keep an eye out for POWs calling for help.

The mini-Boss in the area is a big, mean super tank. It fires at you as it moves around the screen trying to crush you. Time your dashes from one side of the tank to the other, trying also to time the cannon fire. Keep blasting at the sides of the super tank. If you have a secret weapon, use some of it now.

Next, you get to follow the railroad tracks north toward your destination. Watch out for trains—they're armed with cannons and will run you down in no time.

When you get to the next compound, you'll see two cannons in the wall waiting for you. When you've blasted these, the cannons above become active. Only the red plate on the front of the turret is vulnerable.

Past this compound is a three-way fork in the road. You're getting close when you get to the once-paved roadways. The airport route is the hardest. The city is the easiest. The lake route is somewhere between the two in difficulty. If you've already beaten the city route, try the lake route next time. This way you can work your way up to the airport scenes.

Master Tips

❏ Monitor your cannon's power-ups—they are expendable. If you run out of any of them, you could be in trouble.

❏ Combine explosive power with long-range capability for distance fighting. Use V for rapidity of fire when you're in close to the enemy.

❏ The city is not a piece of cake, but it does offer the most power-ups.

❏ Avoid fights whenever you can by going around trouble. You will conserve energy and weapons.

❏ There is no time limit on this game. Often it's wise to simply creep along and take on enemies one group at a time. Don't get so many enemies on screen that you're bound to get nailed.

❏ Enemy tanks are color-coded so you'll know how tough they are.

❏ To take on the enemy headquarters right away, try this password: 2110944.

Bionic Commando

Manufacturer: *Capcom*

Up Front

Bionic Commando is a first class shoot 'em up, with a twist that puts it in a class by itself. The twist is that you have one bionic arm that's attached to a wire. You can use the arm to latch onto objects or cliffs, cross impasses, and even span gaps between buildings. Next to a weapon, a bionic arm is a soldier's best friend.

The story behind this game is quite simple: Super Joe has been captured by the enemy. Your job is to invade the enemy stronghold and whip up on them, getting Joe back in the bargain.

Unlike most war-time shoot 'em ups where you progress from level to level, in Bionic Commando you get a map showing 19 different areas and a helicopter to get you from area to area. Twelve of these areas are battlegrounds—the rest are neutral areas where you're pretty safe. The order in which you take these areas is up to you, but you may need weapons from some areas to be successful in other areas. About all we can tell you is that if you try to take these areas in numerical order, you won't get very far.

Getting Started

To start the game, press Start. Then use the following controls to move Bionic Commando:

⬍◀▶	Move around the screen.
Ⓐ	Use the arrows and button A to move the bionic arm.
Ⓐ	Fire your weapons.

Select the weapons that you will be taking into each zone before entering the zone. If you get into trouble or find yourself in need of other weapons, you can warp out of the action by holding down A and B and pressing Start. You can then change weapons and try again.

Each of the battle areas has a control room that you must find. Find the core in each room and destroy it. Destroy the core and you get new equipment or weapons.

Along the way, you'll come across many doorways. Investigate them all. Some doors lead into communications rooms. If you have the right communicator with you, you can learn several secrets in these rooms. You can get even more information by wiretapping enemy communications. But watch out! Sometimes wiretapping is *wire trapping*—the enemy can learn of your presence and attack you in the communications room. But don't let that keep you from trying—if you miss important communications you won't advance. Besides, if you slip out the door quickly enough, you don't have to fight.

When you first start out, you don't have any continues—if you get blown away, you're dead for good. To earn continues, you must intercept enemy trucks as they move supplies. When you intercept a truck, you land in the chopper and take on a special screen. Certain enemies give up an eagle emblem. Each emblem is equal to one continue.

Our tester suggests the following order for taking on the preliminary stages of the fight.

Area 0

Proceed from Area 0 (your base camp) to Area 1. You have a limited selection of weapons here, but that soon changes. Go underground and find your way to the Core Room. Fight your way to the platform that's on the same level as the core, and stay to the left. Clear out the soldiers behind you. Then begin firing on the core. Soldiers jump down between you and the core. Keep blasting. This technique works for most of the core rooms.

Zone 13

Neutral Zone 13 is your next stop. As you parachute in, you'll see a sentry to your right. Here you can safely test any weapons you just found (these areas are safe in every neutral zone). Once you pass the sentry, however, firing your weapon brings the enemy into the zone. In later areas, you'll meet some bad guys that you want to fight. Lure them into this area and blast them without attracting hordes of enemy soldiers. In this zone, you will find ammo and flares.

Area 4

Area 4 is the next stop in the search for Super Joe. You're going to be searching through caverns, so get ready to use your flares. Make your way into the upper right corner of the maze to find the core. There's only one guy defending this core, but he's got a bionic arm too. The trick is that his arm can't hurt you, at least not in this first encounter. All he can do is knock you around a bit. Ignore him as much as you can. Jump on the platform and blast the core. You will be rewarded the wide cannon, which fires three shots at different angles at once.

Area 15

Area 15 comes next. Find the 1-up on the first door. Use the wide cannon to blast down the wall that blocks the second door. Now the enemy knows you're here. Make a run for the second door and get the communicator.

Area 5

Area 5 brings new excitement in the form of blue balls that don't really hurt you. Avoid them anyway—they can knock you into enemy fire. The leader of this pack is a flying mechanical wonder that guards the core. Get behind it (avoiding the rocket blast that holds it up), and blast the blue part of the generator to destroy it. Now you have the rocket launcher.

Area 2

On to Area 2, and take the rocket launcher with you. Watch out for the blobs of water (and who knows what else) that come out of the pipes, or you'll get swept off your feet. Here come the tractors. They're no match for you and your rocket launcher . . . unless they've dropped their chain. If the chain is down, either wait a minute or get behind them. This area yields the pendant that blocks bullets.

Area 3

Area 3 is next. In this delightful bit of paradise, you must make sure that you don't become dinner for the man-eating plants. Keep an eye on the ground—if it blinks and wiggles, get moving. This area gives you the rapid-fire option.

Area 6

Area 6 is next on your bloody hit parade. This is one tough area to conquer. You'd better be pretty good at using your bionic arm—you'll need to swing out into space, let go, and grab hold before you go splat. Be sure to get the soldiers launching airborne lasers. If you don't blow them away, their weapons just keep on coming. The core guard in this area is a real cutie pie. He has a bionic arm that can hurt you as well as some sort of weird helmet. Only shots to the top of the head will do him in. Hang in there . . . and we do mean *hang*.

By the time you get this far, you should have a good idea of where things are and where Joe is. Or do you?

Moving On

At last you have rescued Joe!

If you thought you were going to get off easy (blasting your way through hundreds of enemy soldiers and making the rescue), forget it. Joe has secret information, and only the two of you working together can save the world from a nasty fate. You and Joe must destroy the Albatross before the enemy can revive the dearly departed Master D. They are trying to complete the ultimate doomsday weapon and only he had (has?) the missing part. Your mission is to make sure he stays dead.

Master Tips

❏ Be sure to talk to the right guy in Area 18. Accept no substitutes.

❏ Neutral zone 19 is a big nothing.

❏ Make sure you visit area 17 and interrogate the prisoner, or you may miss out on the hidden passages.

❏ Remember that you can use your bionic arm as a weapon! If an enemy is directly above you, swat at him with your arm.

❏ To defeat the Albatross, climb up on the engines and blast its little orange heart. Then all you have to do is get out of the base before it explodes. Oh, did we mention the big, BIG chopper? You have to put a rocket through the windshield as you free-fall to an almost certain death! Good luck.

❏ You'll need to experiment a little to figure out which communicators are needed in which areas. Although many of the messages are unimportant, you have to intercept all of them—some are essential.

This group of games requires brains rather than brawn. Included in this category are TV game shows, puzzles, and brain teasers. Also included are board games, such as chess and Anticipation. If you look forward to a good mental challenge, these games are for you.

Quizzlers

Adventures of Lolo

Manufacturer: *Hal America*

Up Front

Take every brain teaser, mechanical puzzle, and riddle that you've ever seen, roll it into a Nintendo game, and you have the Adventures of Lolo. This is one of those games that provides an educational experience without seeming to do so. Lolo makes you look at the obvious and reject it.

When you first start out, you'll think that you've stumbled into something intended for the very young. It ain't so! The simple stuff in the first two levels is just a warm up. By the time you finish, you'll have enhanced your problem solving skills immensely, and you'll have a pretty healthy respect for the game.

Now for the story. The Great Devil has laid waste to the land of Eden and kidnapped the Princess Lala. Lolo has to get her back. Ok, so the plot stinks, but the music makes up for it, at least a little. While the music in most games becomes annoying after several hours, the Lolo theme seems to recede into the background.

One of the most unusual features of this game came to be known by our testers as the *suicide button*. When you realize that you've chosen the wrong solution to the puzzle and there's no way to beat it under the current circumstances, you can press the Select button to give up and start over. Fortunately, the game offers unlimited continues and a password function that lets you pick up where you left off.

Getting Started

To begin the game press Start, unless you want to enter a password. In that case choose the password option and enter the last password from your previous session. Once you're started, use the following controls:

⬍◆▶	Move Lolo through the mazes.
Ⓐ	Fire Magic Shots.
Select	Give up and start over.

The game consists of ten levels of mazes. Each maze is a puzzle all its own. Each of the mazes is a courtyard surrounded by a stone wall and filled with a combination of rocks and trees, sometimes water, Heart Framers (that Lolo must collect), monsters to get in the way, and a treasure chest.

To complete the maze Lolo must gather all the Heart Framers. When he does, the treasure chest opens. As soon as Lolo collects the gem in the chest, the monsters disappear and you can move on to the next puzzle.

Moving On

Two other types of framers come into play. Push the Emerald Framers to block attacks from monsters and to pin them into areas where they can't hurt Lolo. The Special Heart Framers, which look just like the regular variety, give Lolo Magic Shots. With Magic Shots Lolo can turn a certain stationary monster into an egg. The egg can then be moved. When the egg hatches (in about five or six seconds), the monster is positioned where Lolo pushed it. This is an effective technique for blocking the attacks of other monsters. If Lolo puts two Magic shots on the monster in rapid order, the egg is blasted off the screen. But you can't relax—the monster will come back into its original position in about ten seconds.

When you collect a Special Heart Framer, the indicator just under the number of lives will show you how many Magic Shots you have. To use them, wait till Lolo is facing the monster, and then press button A.

Lolo can also push eggs into the river to hop a quick ride . . . if there's a current. Make sure there's a current, though—otherwise, Lolo sinks like a rock.

In the courtyards you'll find a variety of landscaping. There are trees and rocks aplenty. Neither Lolo nor the monsters can pass through trees or rocks. Magic shots cannot pass through them, but watch out—some monsters can shoot through trees. Among the monsters that Lolo will encounter are the following:

Snakey	This little guy is more of a help than a hindrance. He won't attack Lolo. Sometimes he gets in the way, but often you can turn him into an egg and place him between Lolo and real danger.

Leeper	This little greenie falls asleep if he touches Lolo. Often you have to lead him on a merry chase and let him tag you at just the right spot to block danger.
Rocky	Fortunately this pest doesn't show up very often. He looks like a big gray cassette tape. He tries to pin Lolo into corners.
Gol	Moderately harmless, this guy only wakes up after you've taken all the Heart Framers on the screen. When awake, he spits deadly fire. If you stay far enough away, you can outrun his shots.
Skulls	These guys come to life only after all the hearts are gone. If they touch you, say bye-bye.
Medusa	This guy's nasty! Looks like a headhunter, and acts like it too. If Lolo comes into his line of fire, it's all over. Lolo is frozen until the shot hits him. Medusa cannot fire through hearts, Emerald Framers, or monsters.
Alma	This guy bounces back and forth in an area and takes pot shots at you if you get in his way. He too will freeze Lolo like a deer in the headlights. Block him. Stay away.
Don Medusa	The instruction booklet makes this guy sound really bad. He hardly shows up at all. Treat him like a regular old headhunter.

Some mazes have patches of desert sand. Lolo can pass through these areas, but only at half speed. Lava (it looks like red water) is strictly off limits.

Master Tips

❑ If you think that this looks like a simple game, try these passwords to get involved in the later stages:

DHYP

DMYJ

DVYB

Now go back and start from the beginning. You'll need some practice before you're ready for these!

❑ In the final stages of the game you'll encounter puzzles that can only be solved by egging a monster, moving it, grabbing the heart, and then blasting the egg before it hatches. Knowing this doesn't make it any easier.

Anticipation

Manufacturer: *Nintendo*

Up Front

Anticipation is billed as the first board game for the Nintendo system. Up to four people compete to see who can correctly identify a series of connect-the-dot drawings. Four tokens—a pair of shoes, a trumpet, a teddy bear, and an ice cream cone —represent the players. There are four boards, each with yellow, blue, pink, and green spaces. To win the game you must correctly identify at least one drawing per color on each of the boards. This is similar to the way you earn pieces of pie in Trivial Pursuit.

Getting Started

To begin the game select the number of players, how many of the players are to be controlled by the computer, and the skill level desired.

The skill level determines how much of a hint you get for each of the puzzles. The lower skill levels show you the category of the drawing. They also show the dots to be con nected and provide blanks at the bottom of the drawing for the letters of the answer. If you choose higher skill levels, the category, blanks, and/or the dots are omitted, making it harder to solve the puzzle.

At the beginning of the game, each of the tokens is on the same color (yellow) which determines the category for the first puzzle. A screen appears that's broken into two sections—a drawing area and a status area.

The status area contains a die (the singular for dice) that counts down as time elapses. This die determines how many spaces on the board the correct answer will move a player's token. Below the die are drawings of each of the player's controllers. These drawings show who can and cannot buzz in to try and solve the puzzle. If you answer incorrectly, you get locked out for the remainder of that puzzle, while the others have a chance to solve it.

The appearance of the drawing area depends on the skill level you chose and which of the three levels the controlling token is on. At the easier levels, an outline of dots is shown and blanks are provided at the bottom of the drawing area showing how many letters there are in the puzzle. If a higher skill level is chosen, or the controlling token is on an upper level board, the dots and/or the blanks are not shown.

As the puzzle begins, the pencil begins to move around, drawing the lines of the picture while the die counts down from six to one. If you think you know what the drawing is, press your button. You then have a certain amount of time to enter your answer. If you're correct, you get a square of that color. If you're incorrect, the other players are given an opportunity to solve the puzzle. You are then locked out and you can't try again until all of the other players have a chance.

When you give a correct answer, your token is moved the number of spaces shown on the die. A puzzle from that color group is then played. If no player provides a correct answer before the die counts down past one, you get to play another puzzle from that same color group.

Moving On

Unlike most board games, Anticipation does not support the idea of taking turns. Rather, the token belonging to the last correct questioner dictates what color group and level the puzzle comes from. Unless you have already given a wrong answer for the puzzle, you can press your button at any time while the picture is being drawn and the die is counting down.

In the beginning of the game each token starts on a yellow space, so the first puzzle will be from that category. For example, the drawing area will show the category as ALPHABET and show a number of dots in the middle of the screen. The die begins counting down from six as the pencil connects the dots to reveal the picture.

You must be very careful when you get to the fourth board—it contains blank spaces. If you land on a blank space, you fall back to the third board and have to complete it again before you can move up. If you have a comfortable lead, you can use one particularly useful strategy to keep from falling back. Simply let others land on the colors you need on the lower levels, but be careful not to ring in with the die on a number that will send you back down to the previous level.

Master Tips

❏ Be sure to note the category before the pencil begins to move. If the blanks are shown at the bottom of the drawing, count how many there are and how many words are in the answer.

❏ Watch the die. Don't ring in until it shows the number of spaces you need to move to get to the colored space that will take you to the next level. Of course, you run the risk that another player will ring in before you.

❏ If you land on a gray space, your token will rise above the board and begin to spin around the board. The object is to press your button at the right time to make the token land on the color you need. Good luck, it's tougher than it looks.

❏ Be careful how you spell your answer—you get only one wrong letter per puzzle. Enter a second wrong letter and you're disqualified until the next puzzle.

❏ Even in the higher levels where blanks are not shown, a single blank is shown when a player rings in to solve the puzzle. You can use the position of this first blank as a hint, because the answer is always centered under the drawing. The closer the blank is to the center of the screen, the shorter the correct answer is. This may help you decide between two possible answers.

Bomberman

Manufacturer: *Hudson Soft*

Up Front

Bomberman is a slave robot working in an underground bomb factory. One day he hears a rumor that any robot who can make it out of the maze to the Earth's surface becomes human. Well, it doesn't take Bomberman long to figure out that it's worth the risk, so he takes off. Two things stand in his way—all of the rooms he must pass through are bricked up, and they're all full of enemies.

Each of the rooms contains a grid of indestructible concrete blocks. Scattered throughout this grid are bricks that stop Bomberman's progress, hide power-ups, and hide the exit to the room. A clock counts down the time you have left to clear the enemies from the room and find the doorway out.

One charming aspect of this game is that the puzzles are random. There's no way to tell you how to complete room 5, because room 5 is always different. The bricks, hidden door, and power-ups are in different places. The only consistent thing is that the higher the level, the harder it is.

Getting Started

The controller in this game is pretty easy to use:

✦◆	Move around the screen.
Ⓐ	Plant a bomb.
Ⓑ	Activate the remote control in later stages of the game.
Start	Pause the action.

Several different types of panels are contained in the floor of each room—some are hidden. Look for the concrete blocks arranged in a grid. These panels are plain squares and are not affected by bomb blasts. Bomberman can hide behind these to escape the blast from his bombs.

Between the concrete panels are open spaces where Bomberman and enemies can travel or brick panels that can hide any of the other panels:

Bomb—This power-up increases the number of bombs you can set at one time.

Doors—The exit to each room is shown as a set of doors. You must blow out all the brick panels you can in order to find the door.

Power—This item increases the power of the blast produced by the bombs.

Moving On

As you progress through the mazes, you will meet eight different enemies. Each has its own characteristics and ways of moving around the screen. All are deadly, but some are more deadly than others. Each has a different point value ranging from 100 to 8,000 points.

Some of these enemies can pass over brick panels and some cannot. Some are faster than others, and some are more aggressive. You can bet your bolts that the Pontan, who's worth 8,000 points, is fast and aggressive. Some of the enemies simply patrol areas, while others try to come after you. A single touch from any of them will prove fatal to Bomberman.

The mazes begin simply enough. When you lay down a bomb with button A, there's a short delay before it goes off. This gives you time to move far enough away or around a corner to get out of the blast.

In the early rounds, the blast is small and the enemies move slowly. In later rounds, as you pick up power-ups, the action gets faster and faster.

As you clear the room of enemies, you must also lay bombs down where they will blow up brick panels. This clears pathways to walk through and reveals any hidden items under the bricks. Once you've cleared all enemies from the room, use any time remaining to hunt for power-ups and for the exit.

When you've cleared five levels you get a bonus level. The idea here is to get big point totals by blasting the enemies in the room. Unlike the regular game, Bomberman is immune to bomb blasts in the bonus round, so lay down bombs as quickly as you can.

As you progress through the rooms, you receive password codes. You can't continue without the code, so write them down as you go along. That way you can restart from the last level. Forget your password, and you have to start the whole game over again!

Master Tips

❑ Once you've found the door, be careful not to hit it with bomb blasts. If you do, a whole new crop of aggressive enemies enters the screen.

❑ Try to place bombs where they will blast more than one brick panel. Also try to place bombs where enemies are trapped inside the blast zone.

❑ If you can clear all the enemies from the screen with the first seven bombs, you'll rack up some killer bonus points.

❑ Use as much remaining time as you can to find power-ups. As the action becomes harder, you'll need the extra power to get through some of the rooms.

Hollywood Squares

Manufacturer: *Game Tek*

Up Front

Hollywood Squares is another home version of a popular TV game show, which is itself based on the popular home game— Tic Tac Toe.

Like its broadcast brother, the Nintendo version offers players the ability to play a trivia-based game without having to really know the answers. In choosing to agree or disagree with the answer provided by the video stars, players at least have a 50/50 shot at getting the answer correct even when they haven't a clue as to correct answer. Ernest P. Worrell and Albert Einstein would be on a about the same level were they to square off Hollywood style. Know-what-I-mean, Vern?

Getting Started

To start the game, simply choose one-player or two-player mode. If you're by yourself, the computer will provide you with a worthy opponent. Unlike other TV renditions, the computer opponent doesn't lay down and stay out of the way. The very nature of the game (wrong answers give your opponent the square) requires players to do their best.

All of the elements of Hollywood Squares, the TV show, are here except that there are no stars! No Peter Marshall (or sweet John Davidson), no Joan Rivers, no Charley Weaver —none of the Hollywood Stars are present to liven up the proceedings. In their places are a bevy of unknowns, none of whom is nearly as funny as the late Paul Lynde. One might suppose that Game Tek didn't want to pay the kind of royalties it would take to use those high-priced names.

Moving On

The game itself is just like the show. Players choose squares, and then the celebrity occupant of that square provides a joke answer and a real one. Players must decide if the real answer is right by agreeing or disagreeing with the star. Correct responses put an X or an O in the square—the wrong answer gives your opponent the square. Of course, the winning square is never given away—the player must earn it.

Play continues until one of the players gets three in a row horizontally, vertically, or diagonally. A player must win two out of three games to win the match. The game even contains a secret square where you might win a two-week Caribbean vacation for two!

The winner of the match gets to select one of five keys. If that key starts the car, it's yours! The game instructions, however, don't give you an address where you can send off for your prizes.

Master Tips

There is no advanced information for this game. For heaven's sake, this is Hollywood Squares—it ain't rocket science! Go play. Have fun!

Jeopardy

Manufacturer: *Game Tek*

Up Front

Critics have cynically referred to the Jeopardy TV Quiz show as "the only example of high culture on television." More cerebral in nature than most TV offerings, Jeopardy appeals to people whose master of trivia comes from just a touch of book learning.

Game Tek's version of Jeopardy brings it all home with all of the familiar elements that make the TV show so popular. Game Tek even offers a Junior Edition for the younger crowd.

Getting Started

Up to three players can join in the fun of this game, but if you're by yourself or only have one other player, the system will provide the extras for you. The game also offers three skill levels that determine how much time you have for ringing in and answering.

To begin the game, press Select and choose the number of players and the skill level desired. To choose, use the arrow pad to move the highlight to the desired choice and press the red A or B button to select. If you choose fewer than three players, the game asks if you want computer players. Finally, choose the names and characters for your players.

Just as in the TV game there are two rounds of questioning (Jeopardy and Double Jeopardy). Any players who have money left after Jeopardy face off in Final Jeopardy to determine the winner.

Moving On

The main difference between the TV game and the Nintendo version is that spelling counts in the home version. Contestants on TV have the luxury of giving answers orally. Home players, however, must select letters from an alphabet block to form their answers. Fortunately, the question part of the response is given to you so that all answers are "in the form of a question." Don't worry though, you have plenty of time to key in your answers.

The controls in this game are used to select categories and values for the questions:

◀▶   Highlight a category, then press a red button to activate the choice.

▲▼   Choose a particular dollar value in the category.

Unlike the TV show which times the two board rounds, in this version, you can't advance to the next round until all of the questions are answered in this round.

Master Tips

❑ This game does forgive minor spelling errors and typos, but try to get as close as possible. It's hard to tell what the system will accept and what it won't. If you have the time left on the counter, double-check your entries for spelling.

❑ Spaces between words are optional! The game will recognize GlennMiller as Glenn Miller.

❑ Just like the TV version of the game, it's often better to give partial answers. For example, if the answer to a question is Bette Midler, the game would accept Midler but not Bet Midler.

❑ Check the question form supplied by the computer. If the question is What are . . . or Who are . . . make sure that the answer is also in plural form.

❑ When playing against the computer, look for hints. If you don't know an answer, wait to see if the computer will ring in. Often the computer opponent will answer incorrectly by giving an answer that consists of garbage characters (* , ?, etc.) with snips of the real answer thrown in. Read the wrong answer carefully—it may contain just enough of the real answer to jog your memory.

Tetris

Manufacturer: *Nintendo*

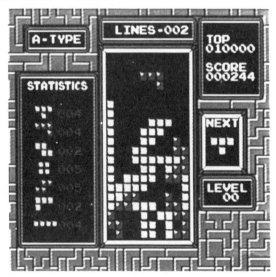

Up Front

Add the name Alexey Pazhitnov to the puzzle makers hall of fame. Tetris is the first popular video game/puzzle to come from the Soviet Union.

The name Tetris is derived from the Greek word tetra, meaning four. If you take four squares and combine them in different patterns, you can form seven different shapes, or tetrads. Sounds simple enough until you play!

You start with an empty rectangular frame in the middle of the screen. Tetrads (the seven different shapes) begin descending one at a time. The object of this game is to combine the tetrads in such a way that they interlock to form a solid line of squares across the frame. Once a line is completed, it disappears, the blocks on top of it fall down to take up the empty space, and the next tetrad begins its descent.

The more lines you form, the higher your score. One of the tetrads that descends is a straight line of four blocks. If you can place this tetrad in such a way that it completes four lines of blocks, you score a Tetris and are awarded big bonus points.

If you liked Rubik's Cube, you'll love Tetris.

You should know that there are two different versions of the Tetris game in circulation for the Nintendo. The version covered here is made by Nintendo. Tengen also produced a Tetris game for the NES. At the time this book was written, the two companies were in a dispute about who actually had the rights to the game in the U.S. If you have the Tengen version of the game, most of the tips and hints presented here will help you play that version as well.

Getting Started

Tetris is one of the only games that lets you choose your music. You have your choice from three different songs or a special setting for no music at all.

You can also choose either of two games. The type A game is a test of stamina with ten different skill levels from which to choose. This game goes on until you have a stack of tetrads built up to the top of the screen. When there's no more room for tetrads to fall, the game is over. The skill level determines how fast the tetrad falls. As the game goes on (if you do well), the skill level is automatically increased until it's raining tetrads.

The B game has a definite goal of building twenty-five lines. Once you have scored twenty-five times or the tetrads have built up so there's no room for others to fall, the game is over. This variation of the game also has ten skill levels as well as an interesting handicap called height. If the height setting is greater than zero, a group of randomly placed tetrads is put at the bottom of the frame—you have to work around them. The higher the setting, the higher the tetrads are stacked. Six different height settings are available.

The screen display is almost identical in both the A and B variations. The B variation shows the height setting and a LINES display at the top of the frame that counts down from twenty-five, showing how many more lines you must complete to win. The A variation does not display height; the LINES display indicates the number of lines you have completed.

Both variations display a statistics window that shows how many of each type of tetrad has fallen into the frame so far. To the right of the frame is a window that shows what the next tetrad to fall will be. It's often useful to check this window—it may determine how you place the currently falling tetrad. If you want an additional challenge, press Select to turn this window off.

Once you choose the type of game you want to play, use the following controls to make your moves:

◀▶	Slide the tetrad from side to side as it falls.
Ⓐ	Rotate the tetrad 90 degrees clockwise.
Ⓑ	Rotate the tetrad 90 degrees counterclockwise.

Once you have the tetrad the way you want it, use the down arrow to make it fall faster. The faster you place tetrads, the higher your point total will be.

Moving On

The most basic strategy is to avoid blocking a blank space with another tetrad. If a blank space does get covered (and it will!), you still may have a chance to get a tetrad into that space. When you complete the lines above that space, the lines disappear, the blanks open up, and you can slip tetrads into them.

If a tetrad covers a blank space from above but leaves the side open, you can slip the falling tetrad sideways when it gets to the bottom—move fast! You can even rotate the tetrad to fill a jagged gap, but you need to do it between the time the tetrad hits the bottom and you hear the thud. Again you will have to be quick on the draw to pull it off.

You can add bonus points to your score in any of several ways. One of the best ways is to complete two or more lines at a time. Finishing four lines at the same time (scoring a Tetris) is worth big bonus points.

You can also score bonus points by lining up the tetrad when it first appears and using the down arrow to make it fall into place quickly. The farther the tetrad falls, the more points you score.

Master Tips

❑ Try dropping your first tetrads down wide end first. This will keep you from building gaps into your lines.

❑ You can usually keep the pile of tetrads under three lines at a time, but remember that a Tetris scores four times as many points as completing three lines with a single tetrad.

❑ To score a Tetris, begin building from one side or the other, keeping the end of the wall one space from the opposite side. When a bar of four squares in a row falls, turn it on end and drop it into the corner for the Tetris and the maximum bonus points.

❑ If you've gotten to level nine with a height of five and you're getting bored (fat chance!), hold down button A and press Start when you are at the level-setting portion of the option menu. You'd better be fast!

Wheel of Fortune

Manufacturer: *Game Tek*

Up Front

If you don't already know how this game works, either you've been in a coma for the last decade or you don't own a TV. The only game show in television history to make a star of a model/hostess makes it's debut on Nintendo! Forget Pat Sajak, he isn't here. But the lovely Vanna is there to turn the letters! Game Tek even offers a Junior Edition for younger players.

This version of the Wheel is as faithful as can be to the TV version. One, two, or three players ride the wheel of fortune, winning money and prizes, and . . . going bankrupt. If you are a player or two shy, don't worry, the game supplies a worthy opponent.

If you are one of those people who sits and guesses the puzzles (don't we all) and wonders why the TV contestants are so slow, here is your chance to put yourself to the test.

Getting Started

To begin play, press Start. The system asks how many players there are. Use the arrow keys to select the number of players.

If you select fewer than three, the system offers computerized competition. You can also choose competition levels from easy to fairly stiff. The players will then be asked to enter their names.

The game presents seven different puzzle categories— Person, Place, Thing, Event, Title, and Phrase. The cartridge stores over 1,000 different puzzles. Unless you play night and day for a week, you'll have a hard time memorizing them. But you can expect some repetition, since the puzzles are selected at random.

When the game starts, the puzzle is placed at the top of the screen. Light colored boxes show where the letters go. In the lower left corner of the screen is a timer. It's on a short fuse, so don't dawdle! If time runs out on you, you lose your turn.

Next to time, the game involves three main activities—Spin, Vowel, and Solve. Cycle between the choices with the left/right arrows, then press one of the red buttons.

First, you will probably choose to spin the wheel. Make sure the word SPIN is highlighted and press a red button. The wheel screen appears with the strength meter moving back and forth (strength controls how long the wheel spins). When the strength is just where you want it, press a red button.

Just as in the real game, you can land on a Free Spin, Bankrupt, or Miss a Turn space, or on a number of different dollar amounts. Where the wheel stops determines the value of your letter guesses.

Moving On

To make a guess, highlight the letters of the alphabet running across the middle of the screen and press a red button. Again, be careful of the time clock. If you run short of time, remember that it's better to make any guess rather than lose your turn. You might get lucky.

You keep spinning until you either make a wrong guess, run into a Bankrupt or Miss a Turn space on the wheel (if you have a free spin you can continue your turn), or until only vowels are left uncovered. If you flub up, the turn passes to the next player.

If you have at least $250, you can buy vowels to fill in some of the missing letters of the puzzle.

At any time during your turn you can attempt to solve the puzzle. To take a chance, highlight SOLVE and press a red button on the controller. The puzzle is duplicated in a window on the bottom of the screen—the dashes represent the covered letters of the puzzle. Fill in the blanks with the letters of your choice. If you make a mistake, the arrow pointing left on the letter line acts as a backspace. When you've filled in your answer, highlight END next to the arrow on the right side of the letter bar and press a red button.

Answer correctly, and the winnings shown for this round are transferred to the winnings box for the match. Remember, tempis fugit! Time flies! The meter's running while you're filling in the blanks.

The player with the most money at the end of the third round gets to play in the bonus round. You can win a new car, a trip to Hawaii, or one of these other fine prizes . . . .

Master Tips

❏ Remember that the most common consonants are R, S, T, and M. These letters are good choices for early guesses.

❏ If you see a word that has only two letters, there's a good chance it's *of, on,* or *an.* Guessing N is a good idea, as the letter may be repeated elsewhere in the puzzle.

❏ The third round is a speed round. Spin the wheel once to determine the value of letters, choose one letter, then guess the puzzle. In this round, you don't have to pay for vowels, but you don't get money for them either. Use the vowels only if you think they'll help you keep the money you already have.

❏ Make your move in the first two rounds—it's hard to get lots of cash in the speed round.

❏ Don't be greedy! Anyone who watches the show on TV can tell you about some poor soul who turned over enough letters so that any fool could solve the puzzle only to spin one too many times and land on a Bankrupt. The next player will thank you, though.

❏ There is no Time Out or Pause button active in this game. The only way to take a time out is to select SPIN and just let the strength meter move up and down while the players get a sandwich.

Role-playing games generally take place in some mythical land. You become the character as you search for items and clues that help you solve mysteries and puzzles to complete your mission. Usually it's mind over matter as strength and bravery take a back seat to a sharp mind.

Role-Playing Games

Castlevania II: Simon's Quest

Manufacturer: *Konami*

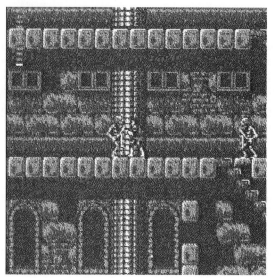

Up Front

If you liked the original Castlevania, or if you're a die-hard Zelda fan, you'll like Castlevania II.

In the original game, our hero, Simon Belmont, slew the evil Count Dracula. Unfortunately, however, everybody didn't live happily ever after. In doing battle with the vampire, Simon inherited his curse. To remove the curse, he must gather together the body parts of the dearly departed vampire, take them to Dracula's castle, and burn them. Only then can Simon rest easily.

Simon must do battle on two different battlegrounds depending on the time of day. During the day, the villages are filled with people and opened doorways invite you in to buy items that will help you on your quest. When night falls, the people leave the streets and the zombies and nasties come out to play.

But never fear—Simon and Indiana Jones have one thing in common, they both are masters of the whip.

Getting Started

You begin your journey armed with the leather whip. Along the way you can get four other whips to give you more power. Buy the thorn whip as soon as you can. Also available are the chain whip, the Morning Star (this beauty has a studded ball on the end that can do some real damage!), and the ultimate flame whip. The flame whip is a magical enhancement of the Morning Star.

Although the game has unlimited continues and passwords to restore you from session to session, try to last as long as possible. The longer you last, the more experience points you earn, making you a more formidable foe.

The basic unit of currency is the heart. As you vanquish enemies they give up hearts that you can use to buy crystals, holy water, daggers, and other weapons. When you lose all of your lives and have to continue, you lose your hearts, so don't be a miser and try to hoard them. When you have enough hearts to buy a weapon, get it.

In the villages and towns you'll meet lots of people. Talk to them. Most of them tell the truth, but a few are not quite trustworthy. Don't forget to talk to the people behind the boarded-up windows. They might have an interesting piece of information.

Some of the people you meet have things to sell you, but you can buy most weapons and treasures in the village shops. These places are easy to spot—they're the only open doors in the villages. During the daytime you can walk right in and talk to the man you find. He will offer you something of value . . . maybe.

The villages also have churches where you can go during the day and refresh your strength. Simon's life force is shown by a vertical bar in the upper right of the screen. When all of the red blocks turn white, you're a goner.

Good luck finding your way. There are no maps available to you. The only directional clues you will get are street signs in the villages—if you know how to read them. Try talking to them!

Your quest begins in the town of Jova. In the beginning of the game you have fifty hearts and the leather whip. Use your first fifty hearts to buy the white crystal.

Hang around till nightfall, so you can get attacked by zombies. As you defeat them, some will give up hearts that you can use to buy Holy Water and the Thorn Whip during the day. Get those items before you start looking for the body parts of Dracula.

Holy Water is one of Simon's most useful possessions. Not only will it stun most enemies, but it can also burn holes in certain stones. This is a good way to find clues and hidden treasures.

Moving On

If you've spent all your hearts or cleaned out a village and it's still daylight, you can always earn a little extra money working your way through the woods and swamps that lay between villages. In fact it's probably better to cross during the day if you can. The darkness multiplies the creatures' power.

When you leave the town of Jova, head to the right through the Jova Woods and toward the Berkely Mansion. The rib of Dracula is hidden there—you can use it as a shield.

The Berkely mansion has a hidden entrance in the form of a floating stone. Hold the crystal to reveal the entrance. The mansion contains many clues and pitfalls. Toss a little Holy Water around—especially into dead ends and most especially into dead ends where deadly stakes block the way.

Beware of the pitfalls. The floor may look solid, but looks can be deceiving. If you have any doubt, toss down some Holy Water. If you hear the sound of breaking glass, the floor is solid. If the bottle goes through, so will you. Some pitfalls are fatal.

The Berkely Mansion sets the pattern you'll see in all of the mansions that contain hunks of Dracula. You'll meet an old man who will sell you an oak stake. You'll need this item to free the body part from the orb that houses it. Once you use the stake, you can't use it again—you need to get another one from the next mansion.

From the Berkely Mansion go to the town of Veros. Come out of the mansion and head to the right. Fight your way through Denis Woods (take the high road and pray that it's daylight), and descend Dabi's Path. Go to the left at the bottom of Dabi's Path and enter the town of Veros.

There you will find several interesting clues, and you'll also have the chance to acquire the chain whip. At 150 hearts it may seem expensive, but boy is it worth it! You may want to spend a couple of nights here collecting hearts, because you can get garlic and laurel here as well. Remember, talk to everybody. If the shops look empty, try a little Holy Water. And don't forget to stop at the church if you're feeling weak. Good town, Veros.

Now that you've got some basic weapons and some magic stuff, you're ready to set out in search for the other missing parts of Dracula. Will we be seeing you at the cremation?

Master Tips

❑ Hidden in the Aljiba Woods is a neat little weapon called the Sacred Flame. The Aljiba is the second patch of woods past the Berkely Mansion. As you're looking around for things, you'll come to two blocks about shoulder height that block your way. Sprinkle them with Holy Water—the Sacred Flame is on the other side.

❏ When you come right out of the the town of Aljiba, you end up at the edge of Yuba Lake. Crouch down by the water, holding your crystal. Surprise!

❏ Stay off the top floors of Lauber Mansion unless you like fighting for your life and little else. All the fun stuff is downstairs. How are you at walking through walls?

❏ In the Belasco Marsh you need the rib and laurel to cross the swamp. You can make it without the laurel, but you'd better be fond of continues.

❏ If you get in trouble, you can't call Transylvania 6-5000. Try to get to a town and stay out of the way of zombies and bats. Yes, there are actually places where you can hide! When day breaks, get into the church for a rest and restoration.

❏ Once you've acquired several weapons and treasures, try getting killed on purpose. This lets you get a password that restores you (minus hearts). Once you have the password you can continue from where you were killed. If you have to use the password later, you will start the journey over again from the town of Jova, and you will have no hearts, but you'll have all of your other treasures.

❏ To cross the Dead River, you need to see the ferryman. Talk to him; he will tell you things. Show him the heart of Dracula and he will take you to Brahm's Mansion where you can obtain the Eye of Count Dracula.

❏ To the left of Brahm's Mansion you jump on floating stones to cross the water. If you jump when the stone is rising, you have a much better chance of getting to the next one. The journey is perilous, but productive—you get a great weapon on the other side. Just remember that it costs one heart to use it.

❏ Garlic and graveyards go together well in Transylvania!

❏ Here are some passwords to play with:

Early: CHFF GPQJ LLM3 TYJK

Middle: RMLP J6F8 GK7F YDZT
         D2RL H4D7 WG7H T8ZX

Late: 7MTM QXFV 1X4J XQJ5

Dragon Warrior

Manufacturer: *Nintendo*

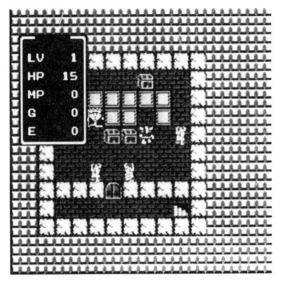

Up Front

Long ago, in the mysterious country of Alefgard, you take on the role of a descendant of the great Erdrick, a legendary warrior who once put the Dragonlord in his place. You must gather all of the ancient items and ancient spells scattered around the countryside to reunite the powers of Erdrick and defeat the Dragonlord.

This is a classic role playing game, steeped in the rich traditions of many of the great computer classics. Where Dragon Warrior differs is in the use of graphics to enhance the action. You might say that this game is the Legend of Zelda without swordplay.

Like Zelda, there is a battery in the game that remembers your status for another day. Unlike Zelda, you can copy a game in progress so that you can try a different strategy or let a friend catch up with you. When you copy a game, all of the character's items and spells are reproduced exactly.

Getting Started

To start a new game you have to enter a name. The game always refers to you by name, even in dialogue. You can enter up to three players. All of the information you get in this game is displayed as dialogue—you can control the speed in which it's displayed. The mechanics of operating this game are simple. Use the arrows to move around the kingdom, and press button A to choose one of the following items:

Talk	See if someone can help you.
Status	Take inventory of your current condition.
Stairs	Go up or down stairs.
Search	Look about for items.
Spell	Cast a magic spell.
Item	Use an item you have found.
Door	Go through a doorway.
Take	Pick up and keep something you find.

Use the arrows to highlight an item. Spell, Item, and Status take you to submenus where you can further refine your choice of action.

Ⓐ	Select an action.
Ⓑ	Cancel a choice.

As you begin your journey, talk to everybody you meet and look inside treasure chests for valuable items. You need to get enough information and tools to start your journey.

As you wander, keep an eye on the window that displays information about your current condition. This window and the Status screen tell you everything you need to know about yourself:

LV (Level)	This is the current level you have achieved.
HP (Hit Points)	When this is zero, you check out.
MP (Magic Power)	Different spells use different amounts of magic power points.
G (Gold)	Gold lets you buy things.

E (Experience)   Points advance you to the
                        next level and are earned
                        by fighting.

Moving On

You begin your quest in the Tantegel Castle. Explore it thoroughly before you leave. You'll find many friends who offer favors for you because they want you to restore peace to the land. Talk to everyone. Anytime you go back to the King and talk to him, he tells you how many experience points you need to reach the next level. He also offers to record your present status so that if you get killed, you'll still have all the items you've found.

Once you've done all you can do in the castle, it's time to move on. One of the people you talked to suggested that you go to Brecconary. Good idea—you can buy weapons there.

The only time you will be attacked is when you are moving through the wilderness. Each type of terrain has its own quirks. In the plains, you can often get through without being attacked. The woods, the hills, and the mountains are each more dangerous than the last. When you're under attack, the game displays a special window that gives you four choices —fight, run, spell, and item. If you choose to fight, a dialogue appears that presents a blow by blow description of the fight. If you choose to run you can escape without the risk of being killed. You can also choose to cast a spell or use an item.

Master Tips

❏ The key to this game is to find all of the items and to build up experience points to gain strength. Each of the spells suggests its use to you. Use them wisely.

❏ Certain spells are better in some fights than others—use the right spell.

❏ Use the Repel spell to keep most attackers away for short periods of time. This usually gives you enough time to get to a town for healing. You hope.

❏ Remember the Wizard in the first town you went to. If you find any cursed items, he's the man to see. These items look like the real thing, but are not at all helpful to you.

- Some people will tell you that a certain treasure is in the castle, and it is . . . sort of. It's in the dungeon! Go around the northeast corner of the castle and go down along the edge of the wall until you come to water. Turn right and go down to find the stairs.
- Erdrick's armor will help heal you and let you pass through the swamp untouched. To get it you must find the deserted town. Go north around the Western mountains, then come south to the desert. The armor is in that town, look high and low for it. Leave no stone unturned. You'll meet some really nasty creatures for the first time. Make sure you have enough experience points to handle it.

Willow

Manufacturer: *Capcom*

Up Front

The action stems from the legend that tells of two gods, the Spirit of the Skies and the Spirit of Earth, who sent messengers to earth to spread peace and joy throughout the world. Bavmorda, the Skies' messenger, became greedy, however, and turned Fin Raziel, the Earth's messenger, into a possum. She then declared herself the Queen of the World. It falls to Willow Ufgood, a member of a miniature race, to destroy the evil Bavmorda and to turn Fin Raziel back into herself.

As Willow, you begin in your own village and make your way to Nockmaar Castle (where Bavmorda reigns). You will meet many friends and enemies and collect a variety of swords, shields, and spells. The object is to build up your strength and your magic until you are strong enough to drive the darkness from the world.

This is a game that takes many days, perhaps weeks of play. When you're done in, you get a password which lets you pick up where you left off.

Getting Started

To begin the game, press the Start button. If you want to continue an earlier game, choose the password option and enter your password. If you are starting fresh, just press Start again. Then use the following controls:

⬍◆▶	Move Willow around the screen.
Ⓐ	Perform the magic spell that you've selected. You can get to the selection screens by pressing Start during the game.
Ⓑ	Use your sword. A quick press thrusts the sword in the direction that Willow faces. Hold down button B to continuously swing the sword.

A controller, such as the NES Advantage, gives you a lot more control—the turbo mode increases the efficiency of your swordplay.

There are several categories or conditions that you will want to pay attention to in the course of the game. The major three are—experience points, magic power, and health points.

As you defeat enemies you gain experience points. The more experience you have, the better you are at defending yourself. As you gain experience points you get promoted through the levels. Levels in this case indicate fighting power, not stages of the game. On the subscreen, the number behind the slash represents how many experience points you need to attain the next level.

Magic points and health points accumulate as you gather spells and items. The numbers behind the slashes on the subscreen show the current maximum levels of these categories. Each time you cast a spell, you use some of your accumulated magic points, and every time you get hit by an enemy you lose some health points. Some places and items in the game will increase and replenish these points.

The subscreen also shows ratings for STR (strength), DEF (defense ability), and AGI (agility). These ratings change depending on your experience and on whether you have a spell, a shield, or a sword. Strength determines the amount of damage you can do with one stroke of the sword. Defensive ability is more or less a measure of your shield. Agility is a rating that combines your current combination of sword, shield, and magic.

Moving On

You begin the game in your own village. Here you are given the magic acorns, a sword, and some valuable advice. Investigate every doorway you can get to—you never know what's inside. Don't worry about the ones you can't get to; they're merely decorative.

Walk up to people you meet on the path and talk to them. They'll tell you their stories and messages in a special screen. To read the rest of the message press A or B. To go through the message quickly (do this only if you already know what the message says), press the up arrow.

Off you go to the village of Dew where you will receive the Wooden Shield. Here you will find news of a man who Bavmorda turned into a monster. This guy preys on the people of his own village. His son will tell you where to find him. Do battle with this monster-man to break the spell. To show his thanks, he'll give you some magic.

Along the way, you'll meet many evil monsters and apparitions. The more enemies you fight, the more experience points you earn, making you a better sword fighter. Of course, it's often better to get around enemies than to fight them, especially early in the game. Build experience points by fighting enemies you know you can beat.

Whenever you fight a boss, energy meters show up on the left side of the screen. E is for Enemy, P shows Willow's power. To defeat the enemy you must use the sword—magic is useless here. Run the enemy's meter to zero and you win.

Pop into every open door and explore every path and cave. You never know where or when you'll find the next great treasure.

Master Tips

❑ Some of the swords you find may be less powerful than the one you already have. Be sure to fit the weapon to the enemy.

❑ When the wind blows, monsters are near.

❑ You must be at least at level 13 to return Fin Raziel to her normal state. Do so as soon as you can, for she is a formidable ally.

❏ To defeat many of the monsters of the forest, stab them then back away so that you can dodge their fire.

❏ Whenever you find an item in a cave, you must make it out to keep the item. If you get killed inside the cave, you must acquire the item again.

❏ At one point you'll turn left near the water and find holes full of chomping teeth in the grass. Use the Specter to avoid death.

❏ Use these passwords only if you lose your own and are in the second half of the quest. If you don't earn the magic yourself, you won't know how to use it properly.

Level 9 e7u 7M8 ?42 1Iy YBe urk

Level 13 Ltf 5KK NA8 Ta! k5v J5A

Zelda II: The Adventures of Link

Manufacturer: *Nintendo*

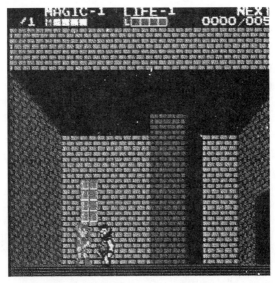

Up Front

The original Zelda had just the right mix of action, adventure, and mind numbing puzzles. The sequel has the same charm. This time, however, Princess Zelda is under a spell. She sleeps more deeply than Princess Aurora. If only a kiss would wake her, but it's not that simple. Link must again take up a quest through the country of Hyrule in search of the third part of the Triforce, Courage.

There are some distinct changes this time around. Instead of having to make your way through a series of mazes, you must explore several towns and six castles to collect your strength and tools. The townsfolk will help you by restoring your energy and by giving you information and magic. Collect enough items and energy to build up Link's powers, and you're ready for the final assault—a rematch with Ganon, the head bad guy of Nintendodom.

Often, gaining magical spells is a two-part process. You must find an item, then present that item to the right person in one of the towns to get the magic.

Getting Started

The game begins in Zelda's Castle where she lies sleeping on the bed. Your character, Link, is there. Use the following controls to move him:

⬍◀▶	Move around the screen.
Ⓐ	Jump!
Ⓑ	Use your sword.
Start	Pause the game. See the items and status menu.

As you travel around the land of Hyrule, you'll cross many different types of terrain. When you travel between locations, you see Hyrule from overhead, like a map. When you enter towns, caves, or castles, or when you get in a fight, the view changes to a normal side shot.

Watch out when you wander off the beaten path—you'll probably get attacked. Lucky for you—you need to fight the evil Ganon's nasty hordes to build up your strength.

As you defeat enemies, you earn points. These points are shown in the upper right corner of the screen. The first number shows how many points you currently have. The second number (behind the slash) shows how many points you must have to get a power-up. Power-ups increase your life force, magic power, or attack power. You have two meters—one shows magic power and the other shows life force. A third measurement, attack power, is also shown in the status area at the top of the screen.

Moving On

Go east from Zelda's Castle. When you enter the forest, just keep going to the town of Raru. If enemies appear, you may be able to dodge or outrun them. If one of them touches you, the screen changes to a side view and you have to fight your way across one or more screens to get back to the overhead traveling view.

Once you get to the town of Raru, use button B to read signs and talk to villagers. They offer valuable clues. Go in every open doorway. Usually there's one place in each town where you can restore your life meter. While in Raru be sure to get the Shield spell.

After leaving Raru, stay on the path going north, then west. You will come to a place where the yellow path, green pastures, and pink desert all come together. Turn directly north across the desert to the cave entrance. You don't have the candle yet, so the cave is in total darkness. You won't be able to see the enemies. Keep a sharp lookout for shadows and such on the floor. At the end of this cave is a trophy. Take it west to the town of Ruto and get Jump Magic.

Once you have Jump Magic you're ready to take on a castle and get the candle to light dark places. Head east out of Ruto and stay on the path. You will see a cave entrance to the north, but the water and mountains stand in your way. When the path turns south, keep going into the woods to the east. You will come to a cave that connects with the one you saw before.

Go northeast and find Papara Castle. When you get there, smash the statue in the front and smash all of the statues inside. Some of them yield useful items.

Explore this castle thoroughly. You need two keys to get to the boss, the guardian of the statue. You can't pass through a locked door without a key unless you have the Fairy magic. When an extra life meter shows up on your screen, you're getting close to the boss. Stay to the left edge of the screen and whack his funny horse head to defeat him.

Once you've cleaned out a castle, it turns to stone and you can't go back in. If the castle doesn't turn to stone, there's still some stuff in it.

Master Tips

❏ Look to the south of the first castle to find a heart container that lengthens your life meter.

❏ Whenever you see odd things on the map, especially odd colored squares, investigate.

❏ Go south from the largest tombstone in the cemetery. Make sure you have Fairy magic to get up the cliff to find a hidden castle.

❏ Find the hidden town. It's in the trees by the water at the end of a cave. If you didn't know better you would think it was just a dead-end. The hammer can chop down trees as well as break stones.

❏ Bagu lives in a hut in the trees. He is the only one who can give you a note that will make the River Man cooperate.

❏ Try climbing things in town.

❏ If you have to break rocks to find a hole in the floor, there must be something down there.

Go ahead, pick your favorite sport—Baseball? Football? Ice Hockey? Professional Wrestling? Chances are, you'll find it here. Shoot hoops with the likes of Michael Jordan and Larry Bird, play a few rounds of golf with Lee Trevino—you can even step into the ring with Iron Mike Tyson! The choice is yours.

Sports Simulations

Baseball Simulator 1.000

Manufacturer: *Culture Brain*

Up Front

Baseball Simulator 1.000 is one of the most thoroughly thought-out sports games we've seen. Not only can you play the usual single game, but you can also create teams by selecting your own players and play a complete season of baseball! The system offers twelve regular teams, six teams that you create, and six Ultra League teams—the superheroes of the diamond.

With these Ultra League teams you can endow players with marvelous, magical abilities. A pitcher can hurl his best pitch, make it stop in mid-air, and then send it flying past the batter. Batters can hit balls that explode when they hit the ground or cause earthquakes so that the best shortstop in the world couldn't field the ball. Our testers called it "Ninja Baseball."

Getting Started

Since this game is so realistic, the options you have may seem a bit overwhelming at first. You'll probably need to look at the instruction booklet a lot the first few times you play this game.

The simplest level offers an exhibition mode where you can select a team and play against the computer or against a friend. Against a friend you can select a best-of-seven series, just like the World Series.

You can also pick a league and schedule an entire season from 5 to 165 games long or create your own league from scratch.

One good way to learn strategies is to choose to watch games that you're not involved in. Or you can save time by having the game compute the winner and move on to the next game. If you and your friends want to play an entire season of ball, each person can choose a team and control that team throughout the season. You'll get to play against each other as well as against some of the computer teams to determine who'll win the coveted pennant. In the Edit mode you can create a whole team made up of your favorite players from the past, present, or future.

If you're familiar with other baseball simulations, you won't have much trouble learning the controls for this game. There are, however, a few subtle differences that you should note:

When Batting

♦♦♦	Position the batter in the batter's box.
Ⓐ	Swing! To bunt, tap button A lightly.
ⒶⒷ	After you hit the ball, use the arrow keys to run the bases. Down is home, right is first, up is second, and left is third. Hold down the arrow key and press button B.

⬍ ◀▶Ⓐ   To return to a base, hold the arrow for that base and press button A.

⬍ ◀▶Ⓐ   Steal a base. You can only begin a steal while the pitcher is winding up. Press the arrow button for the base you want to steal, press button B, then swing as normal.

Ⓑ   If you are using a team with Ultra capabilities, use button B to choose the batter's capability.

Pitching and Fielding

◀▶   Move the pitcher from one side of the pitching rubber to the other.

Ⓐ   To begin the windup, press button A.

⬍   During the windup, press up arrow for a slow pitch or down arrow for a fast pitch. Otherwise, you pitch at normal speed.

◀▶   During the windup, hold down the left or right arrow to aim the ball inside or outside the batter.

◀▶   After pitching, use the left or right arrow key to make the ball curve.

◀   If the pitcher has Ultra capabilities, press the up arrow twice to display the Ultra selection. Use the up and down arrows to cycle through the selections.

⬍◀▶   Once the ball is hit, use the arrows to control the player closest to the ball.

Ⓐ   Jump to catch the ball.

Ⓑ   Dive to catch the ball.

↕ ◀▶Ⓐ   After catching the ball, hold down the arrow
for the base you want to throw to and press
button A.

Moving On

One of the most unique features of this game is the ability to
shade fielders—that is, you can move them to the place you
think the batter is going to hit the ball. This means that you
can shift the outfield toward the first base line for left-handed
batters, or put the shortstop in a little closer to second base
just like big league managers would do.

Either player can press the Start button to call a time
out for pinch hitters, pitching changes, or fielder moves. Once
time is called, press button A to make a change. If you're at
bat, you'll see a list of possible pinch hitters. If you're in the
field, you'll see an overview of the fielders along with a menu
that lets you change the player (substitute, which is how you
change pitchers) or move fielders to put them in different
places. Use button B to return to play.

Master Tips

❏ You can't start to steal a base until the pitcher starts his
windup.

❏ If you're playing an entire season, keep an eye on your
pitchers. When you select a pitcher, you'll see a drawing
that shows the pitcher's emotional and physical state.
The happier he looks, the better he'll perform. If you're
overworking your pitchers, their performance will suffer.

❏ If your team is in first place and leading by more than
five games, your pitching is likely to begin falling apart
due to overwork. Even pitchers that look happy will tire
easily. You'll have to be a good manager to stay in first.

❑ The Ultra capabilities are restricted to Ultra League teams or teams that you have edited yourself.

❑ When you get bored with straight baseball, you can liven things up considerably by getting wacky with Ultra. But don't use up all of your ultra points before your opponent or you'll be at a distinct disadvantage.

Bases Loaded II Second Season

Manufacturer: *Jaleco*

Up Front

If you love the minute details of baseball, the statistics, the mind games, and the smell of stale nachos, this is the game for you!

Bases Loaded II gives you the opportunity to play a complete 130-game schedule against the computer. Win 75 games and you take the pennant and a get a chance to manage in the World Series. At the end of each game, you get a password that lets you continue from the place in the season where you left off.

If you prefer to play against your friends, this system lets you form your own league and play in head-to-head competition. If you create a league, however, you'll need to keep your own statistics on paper.

All of the elements of real baseball are here, including base stealing, wild pitches, bunting, the hit and run, spectacular diving catches, and unhittable pitchers. In fact, about the only thing missing is kicking dirt on the umpire's pants. Sure, you'll get the usual bad calls to make the game seem realistic, but you'll have to settle for yelling at the TV screen.

Getting Started

Like real baseball, the fundamentals are fairly simple. Intricacy comes in the form of execution. (Did Yogi Berra say that? It sounds like something he'd say.)

You have twelve teams to choose from—six in the Eastern division and six in the Western. Each team has a twenty-six man roster. Each player has his own strengths and weaknesses. A complete roster and player statistics are provided for each team.

Before the game begins, you have the opportunity to fine-tune the starting line-up and select a starting pitcher. You will also have to tell the computer what day it is. This enables the NES to compute each player's biorhythm chart. Biorhythms are used to simulate the subtle changes that every real player goes through from day to day. This accounts for slumps and hot streaks.

Biorhythm ratings range from -9 to $+9$ in each category—physical strength, sensitivity, and intellectual capability. Each affects a player's performance differently, and they affect hitters and pitchers differently.

For pitchers, the physical rating determines stamina, which affects speed and control. Sensitivity determines the pitcher's emotional state. Pumped up pitchers throw the ball a bit faster than they normally would. The intellectual rating determines how good a pitcher's stuff is. A pitcher with a high intellectual rating puts more bite into curveballs and knows a little more about a batter's weaknesses. This game follows the Designated Hitter rule, so a pitcher's batting ability is not rated.

For hitters, the physical rating determines overall hitting ability for the day. A high rating means he's hot. The sensitivity rating determines the hitter's emotional state which can affect his long ball chances. Intellectual ratings affect clutch hits—the ability to hit with runners in scoring position.

Moving On

As with most baseball simulators, you use the controller differently on offense (hitting and base running) than on defense (pitching and fielding).

Pitching

To pitch the ball you select different pitches with the arrow keys by holding them down and pressing the A button to start the windup.

From the time the windup starts until the ball hits the catchers mitt, other arrow presses will determine how curveballs break and where fastballs are located. You will need to experiment:

← ↑ Ⓐ	To pitch a fastball outside to a right hand hitter, hold down the up arrow and press A. When the wind up begins, press the left arrow.
Ⓐ	To pitch a change-up (off speed), don't press an arrow when pressing A to start the wind up.
← Ⓐ	To pitch a curveball, hold down the down arrow and press A. Then press the key in the direction you want the ball to break. If you want less curve, release the arrow key some time before the ball reaches the batter.
Ⓑ	Try to pick off a base runner. This causes the camera angle to change to an overhead shot from behind home plate. To throw the ball to one of the bases, hold down the arrow for that base and press A. Right is first, up is second, left is third, and down is home.

Fielding

If the batter hits the ball, the fielder closest to the ball is automatically selected. You can then move that player with the following controls:

⇕◆◗ Move toward the ball.

Ⓑ Jump for the ball. Use the arrow keys with button B to dive for grounders.

Ⓐ To throw the ball, hold down the arrow for the base, and press button A.

Batting

Hitting the ball is one of the most difficult things to do in this game. See, we told you it was like real baseball. Timing is everything, but batters bat close to their published average no matter how well you time things.

Ⓐ Swing!

◆ Swing high.

◆ Swing low.

◆◗ Swing inside or outside the plate's center. Pressing diagonally on the keys causes a combination low inside, etc.

Ⓐ A quick flick of the A button puts the batter in a bunting stance. You can then use the up and down arrows to raise and lower the bat to make contact. You can attempt a surprise bunt by flicking the A button when the pitch is on the way.

Running the Bases

Just as in real baseball, base running is an art:

⇕◆◗ The right arrow controls the runner on first, up controls the runner on second, left controls the runner on third, and down controls all runners simultaneously.

Ⓑ When the hitter makes contact with the ball, press the down arrow and button B to make all the runners advance a base.

Ⓐ To return the runner to a base, press button A and the appropriate arrow key together.

Ⓑ   To take a lead-off, use the arrow buttons and button B while the pitcher has the ball.

ⒷⒶ   To hit and run or to steal a base, hold down the proper arrow and press the B button. Swing with the A button as you normally would.

Ⓐ   To stop a hit and run or a steal, press the down arrow and press A.

Master Tips

❑ Study the pitching statistics in the instruction book that comes with the game. Each pitching staff contains three types of pitchers—starters, middle relievers, and a stopper, the guy they call in to pitch just an inning or two at full tilt boogie. Use your pitchers wisely.

❑ Look at the pitcher's average top speed. If he's got high speed and a low curve percentage, this is your man for bringing the heat. Pitchers with lower top speeds, but higher curve factors are going to be your finesse guys.

❑ If you have controller 1, you can call time out by pressing Start. The umpire behind the plate raises his hand and calls time.

❑ To make a managerial move, press button A. This brings up a list of available pitchers or pinch hitters. Use the arrow keys to highlight the player you want to put into the game and press button A again. To cancel the whole idea, press B.

❑ Mix up your pitches. If you keep throwing the same pitch, the batters will figure it out and take it downtown. Nothing makes a change-up work like a couple of well placed fastballs. By the same token nothing makes a fast ball look so awesome as a few garbage pitches in and around the strike zone.

❑ One of the best garbage pitches is to press the down arrow key for a curveball and start the windup with the A button. While the pitcher's winding up, press the up arrow to place the ball high. As the ball approaches the plate, press the down arrow to make it "fall off the table." Lob it just right and it looks like a softball pitch. Most batters find it irresistible.

❏ Here's another good slow pitch. Hold down the down arrow for the curve, but this time hold the right and down arrows diagonally. The ball curves low and inside by a mile, but for some reason batters go for it in a big way.

❏ Toss a little of this kind of garbage at batters and they will be unable to resist a clean high fast ball.

❏ One of the most interesting pitchers on any team is Reagan, who pitches for (of course) Washington.

❏ Old Dutch is a submarine sidearmer in the style of Dan Quisenberry. Despite his 6.22 ERA, Dutch has one pitch that is almost un-hittable when he's in top form. Hold the up arrow for a fast ball (in the mid seventies range for Dutch), then hold down the right and down arrow keys. The ball drops down and inside almost every time. Usually the pitch is a strike, and if the batter swings, the ball is usually an inch or two below the bat.

❏ If you are having trouble making contact with the ball when you are at the plate, try to keep an eye on the shadow of the ball. Swing just before the shadow crosses from the grass into the dirt in front of the plate. Of course you'll have to adjust this to account for the average speed of the pitches the other guy is giving you, but you may get lucky.

❏ Fielders are generally faster than base runners. If you get a runner caught in a run-down situation and he's fairly close to the fielder with the ball, run after him.

❏ Don't be afraid to juggle your line-up. If a hitter is in a slump, pinch hit for him. If your pitcher is losing speed on his fast ball, start thinking about pulling him. Don't hesitate to make the managerial move—after all, you own the team.

Blades of Steel

Manufacturer: *Konami*

Up Front

Blades of Steel is a real surprise to us. Since all of our testers live in Florida (most of these kids have never seen a real hockey game), it surprised us that so many of them wanted to help cover Blades of Steel, even though many of them referred to the puck as a ball.

Blades of Steel is made by the same company that makes Double Dribble — Konami. The same attention to detail makes this game the class act of its league. While we're not in the business of reviewing or criticizing the games, we have to take our hats off to this one.

It is difficult to simulate team sports on the Nintendo because of the limitations of the system itself. Konami has again succeeded. All of the fast-paced action of real hockey is here. Like the real thing, there are times that the action happens so fast your head spins. It takes intense concentration to be really good at this game.

Getting Started

The options and the way the players control the action on the screen are very simple. When you first start, you get to choose either of two modes of play. The one-player mode pits human against the computer. You can choose just a single game (exhibition) or a tournament at any of three difficulty levels. In the two-player mode, simply choose teams and lock horns.

You can only control one player at a time. This player flashes bright white. When your team has possession of the puck, use the following controls to score goals:

⇕◀▶	Move the player with the puck in any of eight directions.
Ⓑ	Pass the puck in the direction the player is skating.
Ⓐ	Take shots on goal.

On defense the arrow buttons are used to maneuver the defender that is flashing:

⇕◀▶	Move the player on defense in any of eight directions. When the opposing team gets in position to take a shot the arrow keys move the goalie in, out and sideways.
Ⓑ	Switch control to the player who is closest to the puck. You can either go after the puck or skate back for extra defense.

When the offense gets in position to take a shot on goal, a red arrow appears in the crease. The crease is the area inside the box where the goalie sets up. Any shots on goal will go in the direction of this arrow. To block shots, keep the goalie on top of the arrow as much as possible.

Moving On

Penalties are rare in this brand of hockey, but there are a few. Icing occurs when you pass the puck across both blue lines (from your end of the ice) and across the line at the opposite end of the rink. If the opponent touches the puck first, icing is called, and there's a face off.

Of course you'll have some fights! Hockey wouldn't be hockey without a little extracurricular activity. When a fight begins, the two players go to it. The loser gets pulled off the ice (allegedly being called for a penalty) and the other team has a one man advantage (power play) for a short period of time.

To fight, use the B button to punch and the A button to cover up. Use the up and down arrows to select a punch to the head or a punch to the midsection. Sometimes, however, the referee breaks up the fight before it begins. He calls a penalty and one of the players gets to take a penalty shot.

The penalty shot is one-on-one against the goalie. Aim the shot with the arrows and let it fly with button A. The goalie can try to block the shot using the arrow keys and button A. This same screen is used for shoot-outs when the game ends in a tie.

Tie games are decided by shoot-out. First, there's a best of five. If the game is still tied, the players go into a sudden death shoot-out—first score wins.

Master Tips

❑ The trick to winning this game is to pass the puck until you get a clean shot on goal. When the goalie moves off the bouncing arrow, take the shot.

❑ If you have the lead late in the game, delay. Take the puck back into your own end and run the opponent's lone defender around the goal. Every time he gets hit by the goalie or runs into the mouth of the goal, he falls down. If you want another skater to come back so you can pass the puck, move toward the blue line. One of your teammates will come skating into the picture.

❑ When you're goalie starts working, you don't lose control over your flashing defender! You can bring him into the crease to help out on defense, although you may get in the goalie's way.

❑ If the offense is taking a long shot, stay with the defender longer—you'll still have time to get the goalie into position over the arrow for the block.

❏ When you're on defense, watch the arrow—this tells you where you need to move the goalie to block the shot.

❏ Even the pros take a lot of shots on goal to score a few points. Don't pass the puck around so long that you make a mistake and turn it over. Try to set your shots up, but don't be so shy about taking the shot that you lose the puck for lack of trying.

Double Dribble

Manufacturer: *Konami*

Up Front

There are a number of basketball games on the market, but Double Dribble is one of the old veterans. If you want a pure basketball simulation without having player personalities superimposed on the game, this is the one for you.

Double Dribble has only one minor drawback—the screen gets so busy at times that the screen starts to slip. At times you'll see a player floating down court without legs. Of course this isn't entirely the game's fault—the Nintendo system itself is known for going into overload when many objects are moving around at the same time. And sometimes Michael Jordan himself seems to move down court without legs!

Once you get past this minor shortcoming, you'll have a lot of fun with this game. Unlike some other types of games that get boring the first time you beat them, Double Dribble holds your interest because the game is as exciting as your opponent's skill.

This is one fast-paced game! Because of their faster reflexes, kids will usually be able to beat the adults. Sorry, Dad, but Junior will probably be able to get position and drop a thirty-foot rainbow before you figure out which button you need to push.

Getting Started

You can play Double Dribble against the NES in one-player mode or compete against a friend in the two-player mode. In one-player mode, you can choose any of three different skill levels for your computerized opponent.

To get the game going, choose either mode of play. On the option screen that appears, each option is represented by a basket. You make choices by shooting the ball through the basket. Use the up and down arrows to choose the option and press button A to shoot a basketball through the hoop. Each time you shoot a particular option's basket, it cycles to the next possible setting.

The first option you have is to set the length of the periods to five, ten, twenty, or thirty minutes. Of course these are not real minutes, the clock moves faster than a real clock would, but it enables you to change the length of the game.

There are four available teams—Los Angeles (the best overall players according to our testers), Boston (the computer is always Boston in the one-player mode), Chicago, and New York. Our testers say that New York is a weak team—if you're playing against someone who's a lot better than you, have them pick New York to even the sides.

In the one-player mode, one of the baskets is used to set the skill level rather than to pick a team for the computer. Remember the NES is always Boston.

Once the options are set, drop a ball in the END basket and watch the crowd file in for the tip off.

Moving On

The controller works differently depending on whether your team has the ball (on offense) or is defending the basket.

Offense

⬍ ◀▶	Change the direction of the player with the ball.
Ⓐ	Pass the ball to a teammate in the direction you're facing. The player that will get the pass is flashing.
Ⓑ	Jump to shoot. Release the button to release the ball. You must release the ball before the player comes down or you'll be called for traveling and you'll lose the ball.

Defense

On defense you only control one player. The other players on the team play man-to-man defense on the remaining players.

Ⓑ   Change the player you're controlling to the player closest to the ball.

Ⓐ   Try to steal the ball when you're close to it. Use this button also to block a shot. Even if you miss the block, you can cause the shooter to miss by getting up in his face.

When you take a shot close to the basket, you will often get to see the shot in slow motion on the Nintendo "Slam-Cam." This particular piece of graphic work is really spectacular although you miss more dunks than you would see in a real game.

The computerized (invisible) referee will call several different fouls, including pushing, blocking, and traveling. As in real basketball you must advance the ball into your half of the court within ten seconds, and you cannot pass the ball back over into the other half of the court (back passing) once the ball has crossed the time line. The ref will call these violations as well.

If you get possession of the ball on an out-of-bounds, because the opponent scored or because of a traveling call, you have five seconds to inbound the ball. If you don't inbound the ball within five seconds, you lose possession.

When you go to take a foul shot, you will see a ring bouncing over the rim of the basket. This is Double Dribble's equivalent of ten thousand fans chanting, "Airball!" To sink a free throw, time the shot to begin when the ring is closest to the basket. The closer they are together, the better the odds of your shot going in.

Master Tips

❑ Release the ball at or near the top of your jump.

❑ Whenever possible, get close enough to your opponent's shooter to attempt a block. Even if you miss, you might throw him off.

❏ When playing against the computer, pass the ball quickly and frequently. The computer is really good at stealing the ball. The more you pass, the less chance the computer has to steal off your dribble.

❏ Work the ball inside for short shots.

❏ Brush up on your three-point shooting. Avoid the middle distance shots as much as possible. Rain them in from the outside or jam them in from under the basket.

Excitebike

Manufacturer: *Nintendo*

Up Front

At first glance you don't expect much from this motocross simulation—you're just racing your motorcycle around the track. In its simplest form, younger players can get a real thrill out of it.

But the game can get pretty challenging for older players as well, because it lets you design your own track! Think of the possibilities. You can design motocross tracks the way Jack Nicklaus designs golf courses—tight, mean, and difficult.

Getting Started

The opening screen includes two different modes for running the pre-designed tracks. Mode A lets you be the only bike on the course. You compete against the clock. Mode B puts you in competition with other riders.

In reality you're not really competing against the other riders since one of these guys will almost certainly cross the finish before you. The other riders simply add an extra degree of difficulty, trying to knock you down and get in your way. Controlling the bike is really simple:

Ⓐ   Go!

Ⓑ   Turbo mode—go faster!

⬍   Steer the bike toward the top and bottom lanes of the track.

◀   Pull the front wheel off the ground for wheelies and jumping.

The nasty thing about turbo is that it will overheat your engine (a temperature gauge is shown at the bottom of the screen). To avoid overheating, release button B and keep running with button A, or run over the arrows painted on the track that cool down your engine. When you kick into turbo mode, you'll hear an especially mean sounding engine noise. Just before you start overheating, you'll hear a warning beep. If you ignore this beep, your engine will overheat, and you'll have to sit on the side of the track for awhile to cool down.

If your front wheel gets hit by another rider, you miss a jump, or run into an obstacle, you may get thrown from the bike. It will take you a few seconds to climb back on and get underway—you'll definitely lose your lead.

You'll have to run through a series of pre-designed tracks. As you master one and make it to the winner's stand, you graduate to the next (harder) track.

Moving On

The real charm of this game is that you can design and save your own track. This way you can challenge your friends and family to a grueling motocross obstacle course.

To design your own track, choose DESIGN from the starting screen. This takes you to another screen that has several different options. At the top of the screen are options for play modes A and B. If you do not have a custom-designed track loaded, these modes make an excellent practice area for learning how to handle the bike—they give you a nice smooth track.

At the bottom of the screen is a frame that contains the design features of the game. DESIGN lets you build a track to your own specifications. SAVE lets you save your design for another day. LOAD lets you use a previously designed track. RESET takes you back to the opening screen. (RESET does exactly the same thing as hitting the RESET button on the front of the Nintendo system.)

To design a course choose the DESIGN option and press Start. The rider advances a little from the starting line and stops. At the bottom of the screen are the letters A through S along with the abbreviations CL, END, and LP.

Use button A to advance the rider to the spot where you want to place an obstacle (designers prefer to call them terrain features), and move the arrow under a letter, then press button B to put the obstacle on the course. If the obstacle is not quite what you want, just change letters and press B again. Here are what the letter codes mean:

A-G	This is the largest group of obstacles, made up mostly of bumps and ramps. A is the smallest and G is a monster jump.
H	H places small jump ramps on a steep angle.
I-J	I and J place straight up barriers on different sides of the track that riders must change lanes to avoid.
K-L	These two put oil slicks on the track.
M-N	M and N put stripes on the track that reset the temperature gauge of any bike crossing them. These keep bikes from overheating.
O-P	These choices replace the track with grass, narrowing the track to two lanes. Bikes slow down in the grass.
Q	Use Q to put grass patches across the whole track. These are especially nasty just after a jump. If the rider doesn't clear the jump all the way, the grass holds them up.
R	This is the tallest obstacle available. The testers called this one Mount Everest.
S	This obstacle consists of a tall jump with a long above-ground ramp on the top end of the track. Riders have their choice of taking the jump on the low end of the track or hitting the ramp on the top end of the track.
CL	Clears whatever obstacle is on the track.
END	Puts down the finish line.
LP	This counter is used to specify the number of laps in the race. Valid lap counts go from one to nine.

When you've finished designing a track, you can run it using either the A or B mode. If you like what you have built, you can save it to the game for another day with the SAVE option from the menu screen. To run a track that you have saved previously, choose LOAD. To modify the track, choose DESIGN again.

Master Tips

❏ When racing against other riders, try knocking them out of the way by cutting right in front of them and hitting their front tire with the back end of your bike.

❏ After a jump, land with the wheels level or with the front end up. If you hit with the front wheel first, you'll be eating dirt.

❏ Reserve turbo mode for those times when you really need it. Turbo gives you a nice springy jump or lets you get ahead of another bike so you can chop his front tire out from under him.

Hoops

Manufacturer: *Jaleco*

Up Front

If David Letterman were to review this game he might say, "This is more fun than should legally be allowed." We don't know if Dave has even seen Hoops yet, but this game is Indiana half court in its finest tradition. And you know how they like their roundball in Indiana!

Very simply stated, Hoops is rough and tumble alley basketball. There are eight different players that you can choose, each with a slightly different set of skills. The combinations are nearly endless. You have your choice of playing one-on-one or two-on-two against the computer or against a friend. Playing against a friend is more fun because the computer player doesn't throw things across the room when you score a really tough point.

Getting Started

To begin the game, press Start. Use the arrows to choose one-player or two-player mode, or you can choose to watch. The WATCH option lets you view a completely computer-controlled game so you can pick up some hints and techniques. You can only use the CONTINUE option in two-on-two games.

Next, you are given an opportunity to choose the game mode. Options include one-on-one games or two-on-two games against the computer or against each other. The two players against the computer gives you an interesting, fast-paced game.

Once you've selected the type of game you want, choose up sides. Use the select mode to put a player on your team, and use the profile mode to find out more about a player's characteristics.

In the two-on-two game, the person using controller 1 selects one player, then the opponent gets to pick. The process continues until the sides are complete.

You also have a chance to determine how many points it takes to win the game (10, 15, 20, 25), who gets the ball when a point is made (winners-out means the team who scores brings the ball in), and where the court is—East or West. The court makes for very subtle differences in the game, just like a home-court advantage.

You have two options for determining who gets the ball first. You can shoot it out, or go around-the-world. Either way you must time your shot with an arrow bouncing around the rim of the basket in order to sink the shot. Don't worry, this arrow foolishness goes away as soon as the game begins.

Moving On

Like real schoolyard ball, you don't have to fuss with a whole lot of rules. Just get down to business. Use the following controls to make your move:

⬍⬌	Move the player around the screen. In two-on-two games the player you're controlling has a number over his head. The computer controls the other player.
Ⓑ	Jump and shoot. Press B once to jump, and again to shoot.
Ⓐ	Pass the ball. If you're playing two-on-two, press A while you're in the air to jump pass to the other player. If you go up for a shot and fail to press either A or B, you'll be called for traveling.

Offensive charging and defensive pushing are the only other fouls that the computer calls. Any of these fouls calls for a change of possession. There are no free throws.

If you are close enough to the basket and shoot, the game shows a close up of your slam dunk. Where this game shines is the way dunks are handled. If a defender is close, you'll see them in the close up trying to block the dunk. A slam is far from automatic in this game.

Half court basketball has always meant ferocious defense. Hoops is no exception. Use button A on defense to spread out and take a "go around me" stance. If you're close enough, button A attempt to steal as well. Some players shine on defense and will unexpectedly steal the ball without any action from you.

Master Tips

❏ If you take your team through fifteen wins against the computer in a tournament, you'll learn a lot more about the players. (Hint, hint, secret stuff!)

❏ In a one-on-one game, select a fast player. Quite often you will be able to get inside for an uncontested slam.

❏ In the two-on-two game you need balance. Choose a playmaker and a speed demon for the best balance. The first player you select inbounds the ball when your opponent scores. Choosing your slower player first lets you inbound more successfully, because your faster player can get open. If you time the pass well enough, you can get a fast break and a slam out of it.

❏ Each player has a favorite place on the court to shoot from. Learn each player's spots. This will help you on offense and will help you to defend against that player. Watching a game where the computer controls all of the players is a good way to get this information.

❏ The jump pass can be a very effective weapon. Press B as though you're going up to shoot, then press A to pass. Many times this freezes the defense for a second (especially if you are playing a human opponent) and you can drive the lane.

❏ When your opponent goes up for the slam, go up with them. If you're close enough, you have a good chance of blocking the shot. The percentage of blocked shots goes way up when the defender is taller than the shooter.

Jordan vs. Bird: One on One

Manufacturer: *Milton Bradley*

Up Front

One on One is really three games in one. You have the three-point contest, the slam dunk, and, of course, the featured event, Michael and Larry going one on one.

Begin learning the game by trying the three-point contest. Here you will learn the fundamentals of shooting. Next, try the slam dunk to learn how to control the players on the court. Once you have mastered these skills, you are ready to take up the gauntlet and go one on one with the masters of the game.

Getting Started

Press Start to get past the opening screen. The selection screen comes up offering you three variations of one on one, three variations of slam dunk, and two variations of the three-point contest. Use the arrows to make your selection and press Start.

The three-point contest has a warm-up mode so that you can practice your shooting without a time limit. The game itself lets up to four players compete against each other. The one-player game pits you against the computer.

The slam dunk contest is a bit more structured, offering ten types of slam dunks. Each dunk is slightly different, with a specific take-off point for each. A panel of judges scores the contest, giving up to ten points each for a total of 50—a perfect dunk. To learn the dunks, try follow the leader. A computer-controlled Michael will demonstrate each dunk for you, then you get to try.

You can play the slam dunk contest with up to four players. After each round, the low scorer is dropped from the game and play continues until only two shooters are left. High score wins.

The feature game on this cartridge is Larry and Michael going at it in a wild half court shoot-out. Each of the real player's styles and tendencies is built into the program for a more lifelike simulation. And you can choose from several variations of the game. You can either play four quarters of variable length or you can play to 11 or 15 points. You decide whether or not fouls are called and who gets the ball when points are scored.

Moving On

Since this game cartridge has three games, let's look at each game in turn.

The Three-Point Contest

The three-point contest is a good starting place to learn shooting techniques. To shoot the ball press button A. This begins the shooting motion. To release the ball, release button A at or near the top of the jump.

Five racks of balls are distributed around the three-point line. Each rack contains five balls. Each shot made is worth one point, except for the last ball on each rack, which is worth two. You have sixty seconds to make all the shots you can. Your player begins in the right corner, but you can shoot from each of the racks in any order you like.

There's one thing to watch out for in this game. Only one ball can be in the air at a time. If you try to shoot too quickly, you will cancel the previous shot before it gets to the basket. Wait to see if the ball scores before starting the next shot. On the other hand, if you see that the ball is going to miss, don't wait for it to hit the floor. Go ahead and shoot the next ball.

The Slam Dunk Contest

The best way to learn slam dunks is to play follow the leader with Michael. He demonstrates the dunk. Watch for the take-off point and the body position when he lets go of the ball. You then have the opportunity to try the same dunk. See what the judges give you. When you start scoring consistently high marks on the dunks, you are ready to take on a friend, or maybe even Jordan himself.

One on One

The real reason for this game is the one-on-one game between Larry and Michael. You have three options—full game (which is timed against the clock), 15 or 11 (the first to score either 15 or 11 points is the winner), and the warm-up where you can learn the player's moves.

When you choose your game, you will be taken to the set features screen. Use the arrow buttons to select which feature to adjust and button A to cycle through the possible choices.

If you are playing against the computer, you can choose one of four levels ranging from 4-Schoolyard to 1-Pro. The lower the level number, the harder the game is. On the easier levels you get three points for a shot outside the line and two points inside the line. On the harder levels you only get two points from outside the three point line and one point for anything shorter. This favors Bird, who is a great three-point shooter, but Jordan gets a bit quicker in the higher levels to make up for it.

Winner's out means that the player who scores gets the ball again. This is a hard game because you can fall behind quickly, and stay that way.

You may want to start with a no fouls game. That way you won't lose the ball on blocking and charging fouls.

You also can control the length of the periods in the full game mode.

To move players, use the arrows alone and in combination with button B. To attempt a steal, use button B alone. Use button A to shoot.

Master Tips

❏ The two players have very different styles. Jordan is fast and sneaky and sinks the close ones. Bird is a bit more methodical, is an excellent rebounder, and can sink the long ones.

❏ To win with Michael you must play an aggressive, in-your-face kind of a defense and drive the lane for the automatic dunks (you won't even need to release button A for dunks).

❏ Michael's biggest weakness in this game is his outside shooting. Larry is a much better rebounder. Michael can steal the ball by going up with Larry at the shot, especially if he's close. This is about the only way to lower Larry's shooting percentage.

❏ To win with Larry keep Michael in front of you on defense. If you let him past you, he scores. Stay close, but stay between Michael and the basket. On offense take the open three-pointers.

❏ If Michael is right in your face, get away. Michael is very good at stealing the ball at the top of the jump. The farther out you keep Michael, the lower his shooting percentage.

❏ Use the bottom of the screen as a teammate. When you get the ball to bring it in, your player is very close to the bottom of the screen. If, on defense, you can force your opponent all the way back, his only moves are side to side. There are times you can use the back line to draw a charging foul and a change of possession.

❏ If you advance the ball with your back to the defender, you are less likely to draw a charging foul.

❏ Fake a shot. If the guy goes up to block it, move to the side and take the jumper. Both players have good shots when they're in the clear.

Lee Trevino's Fighting Golf

Manufacturer: *SNK*

Up Front

By definition, the game of golf involves the use of two balls. The first is 1 1/4 inches in diameter, the second is 25,000 miles in diameter. The object of the game is to insert ball number one into ball number two. No problem . . . till you try to do it.

Lee Trevino's Fighting Golf is one of the best names to be given to a Nintendo game in a long, long time. You definitely need to fight your way over each fairway in this detailed simulation of one of the world's most maddening sports. Play a Nassau round with one of the computer-controlled players, and you'll know how it feels to get the pants beaten off you by Trevino himself.

Fighting golf comes with your choice of two extremely challenging courses. First is the American course that features long par fours, lots of sand, and plenty of the roughest rough you'll ever encounter. The second course is a Japanese design. Land is at a premium in Japan, so the course is shorter, but it sure isn't any easier! The Japanese course has enough water hazards and bunkers to drive you plenty crazy.

Fighting Golf supplies four different players, whose roles you can assume. Of course Mr. Trevino himself shows up in the guise of Super Mex, an all around player who hits the ball an average distance but very accurately.

Pretty Amy is the tour's only female player. She's not a master of the long ball, but she makes up for it with accuracy.

Big Jumbo is the power hitter of the group. His power is just short of Iron Byron's, the perfect swinging machine used to test golf balls for maximum distance. (This machine was named after Byron Nelson, a legendary long-ball hitter himself.) Jumbo is hard to control because his swing is so fast.

The foursome is rounded out by Miracle Chosuke, inventor of the *Reverse Miracle Putt*. His power is just under that of

Super Mex, but just when you think he's missed his putt, things happen that you've only seen in movies like *Caddyshack*!

Lee Trevino's Fighting Golf provides you with hours of fun. It's a nice break from some of the more frantic shoot 'em ups.

Getting Started

To begin playing Lee Trevino's Fighting Golf, first select the number of players and the type of the match. Two types of matches are available—regular stroke play and the Nassau. Stroke play is just the same as you have seen in televised golf tournaments. The player with the fewest strokes over eighteen holes wins.

The Nassau, on the other hand, is a betting game—the winner of each hole gets ten points. Usually these points are converted into dollars in the clubhouse after the match. You can really loose your shirt! On the last hole, the player who is behind can "press," which is a fancy way of saying "double or nothing." In this version of the game, you also get trophies for longest drive and nearest the pin on selected holes.

Select the course, and you're on your way. A practice tee is thoughtfully provided so that you can practice your swing. Start with the American course. It's much more open and forgiving, even though it's longer. The Japanese course is tighter with many more water hazards. Remember, a ball in the water counts as a penalty stroke plus the stroke used to hit the ball. Water penalties can add up quickly on the Japanese course, not to mention the expense of all those lost balls.

Before each hole, the game shows you a map of the hole, along with hints on how to play the hole like a pro. To play any hole successfully, you need to master two basic swings— course play and putting.

To hit the ball with either a wood or an iron, press button A three times. The first press starts the backswing, the second starts forward motion, and the third determines how squarely you hit the ball.

A bar meter just below the player's feet shows you the progress of the swing. Press button A the first time and the meter moves to the left, showing how far you're going back. The longer your backswing, the stronger and longer your shot. When the meter shows the backswing you want, press A again to start forward motion. An arrow in the middle of the meter shows where you'll make perfect contact with the ball. If you press the button the third time before the arrow, the ball fades (curves to the right). If the meter goes past the arrow, the ball draws (curves to the left). If the meter stops right on the arrow, the ball flies straight and true.

Fades and draws are often handy for getting around trees or curling the ball up onto a selected spot on the fairway. It takes practice, but once mastered it will take strokes off your game.

Putting requires only two presses of the A button. The distance the meter moves between the two presses determines how hard you hit the ball on a putt.

Moving On

One of the charms of Lee Trevino's Fighting Golf is the detail that's been put into the game. You must not only develop your skills, but you must also fight the course and the elements to succeed.

There are four types of rough to deal with when you miss the fairway, and you will miss the fairway quite often. Just as in real golf, the deeper the rough, the harder it is to get a clean shot out of it.

In the upper-right corner of the screen is a wind indicator showing you the direction and speed of the wind. Remember that the speed is shown in meters, so that a 3M crosswind is actually about a nine mile-per-hour crosswind, more than enough to affect the flight of the ball. Depending on wind conditions you may want to hit the ball high (lots of arc) or low. To hit the ball high, hold down the up arrow on the controller as you take your shot. If the wind is at your back, this will give you some extra distance as well. To hit the ball low, hold the down arrow while shooting. If the wind is in your face, this will keep the wind from driving back your shot.

When it's your shot, the computer automatically aims and selects a club for you. You can change these choices with button B. Press button B once to view cross hairs that show where you're aiming the ball. The computer always aims straight for the hole, but there may be obstacles in the way that you want to go around. Move the cross hairs with the arrow pad.

To change clubs, press button B a second time—your club indicator will start to blink. Use the left arrow to choose more club and the right arrow to choose a shorter club. You'll need to experiment at first to figure out which club is right for each situation. Shorter clubs are more forgiving—they'll give you straighter shots even if you miss the square shot arrow by a mark or two. Woods and long irons (the lower the number the longer the club) are less forgiving, but generally make the ball go farther.

Before you press button B the third time (to take your shot), you can press A to see different views of the hole you're playing.

Shots from the bunker require a delicate touch. Anything less than a perfect shot will cause the ball to travel a much shorter distance than you might expect.

At any time during your shot, you can press the Select button to display the scoreboard and see how well you're doing.

Master Tips

❏ When you get close to the green, you can apply backspin to the ball to keep it from rolling so far. Hold down the left or right arrow key while you make your shot. The shorter your backswing, the more backspin you'll give the ball. You can simulate those pretty shots that you see on TV where the ball hits the green then rolls back toward the cup.

❏ In real golf, half the game is putting. Lee Trevino has often been quoted as saying that, "You drive for show, but you putt for dough." The same is true of Fighting Golf. Once on the green you'll see patterns in the grass that form arrows. These arrows show you how the slope of the green will make the ball break. The trick is to judge how hard you must hit the ball, and to which side of the cup you must aim to sink the long ones.

❏ Some greens break in more than one direction. If the arrows are pointing toward the ball, your putt is uphill—hit the ball a little harder. If the arrows point away from the ball and toward the cup, hit softly or you may end up on the other side of the green.

❏ It takes a cool head, a keen eye, and a quick hand to excel at Fighting Golf. So practice, practice, practice.

Mike Tyson's Punch-Out

Manufacturer: *Nintendo*

Up Front

In Punch-Out, you take on a series of challengers. You must win a minor championship and several rematches before you can take on the ultimate champion, Mike Tyson, himself. In every fight you are out-muscled by larger more aggressive fighters. Some are easy, but some can tear your head off.

By the way, your old friend, Mario, is moonlighting as a referee now.

Getting Started

Boxing is a game of quick moves. You'd better dodge when the opponent is trying to land the big one, and you'd better be quick with your jabs. Use the following controls to fight:

◆◆	Dodge your opponent's blows.
◆	Aim a punch at the opponent's head. Otherwise, you throw a body punch.
Ⓐ	Throw a right.
Ⓑ	Throw a left.
Start	Throw an uppercut if you have collected any stars.
Select	Listen to Doc, the trainer. This will increase your stamina.

Keep an eye on the status board above the ring, at the top of the screen. The board contains two stamina meters—one for you and one for your opponent. There is a time counter that shows how much time is left in each round as well as a point total that determines the winner if the fight goes to the judges for a decision.

Hearts are very important. Little Mac must have one or more hearts to be able to punch. Each time he throws a punch and misses and each time he gets hit, he loses a heart. If he has no hearts, he changes color. You have to dodge and duck to keep from being knocked silly.

You can get up to three stars during the bout. Stars give Mac the ability to throw jaw-breaking uppercuts. If he gets punched, he loses a star. If he gets knocked down, he loses them all. Get them and use them. As Doc says, "They don't grow finer with age, son."

Moving On

Your first few opponents are real characters. Here's a rundown to give you some idea of what to look for.

Glass Joe

This one's a cake walk. Use Joe to learn the ropes. He's a real patsy with a glass jaw. Keep in his face. When he does his little dance, sock him in the jaw. Down he goes!

Von Kaiser

Von Kaiser is a straightforward fighter. When he leans to one side, give him body shots on the side he's leaning to. When he stands up and says, "Augh Augh Augh," you know you've got him. Smack him one with an uppercut and he'll be seeing birdies.

Piston Honda

This guy telegraphs better than old Samuel Morse. He will back off and bob and weave. When he comes back at you, sock him one right in the puss. It might be enough to put him out for the count.

Don Flamenco

Let this guy throw the first punch. If he misses it, start in with the old left-right to the head. Keep punching his head, but watch out for his uppercut.

King Hippo

When he opens his mouth, put a glove in it, then work the body over real good. Rinse and repeat. He'll go down hard.

Master Tips

- ❏ Watch your opponent's stamina meter at the end of the first round. If it's next to nothing, he may not get anything back between rounds. One good punch might put him away.

- ❏ The trick with the Select button between rounds only works once in a fight—use it wisely.

- ❏ With some fighters, you can't win a decision, even if Mario is on your side. Knock these guys out.

- ❏ When you see a fighter for the second time, rest assured that he has been training hard for you. You may have to adopt a slightly different strategy to beat him the second time around.

- ❏ The number of hearts you start the fight with is a pretty good indication of the kind of power your opponent has. Lots of hearts usually means this guy can take a punch and dish out a few of his own.

❏ Mr. Sandman is about the toughest fighter there is. Our tester says he has more trouble with Sandman than he does with Mike Tyson. The only way to beat him is to slip his punches and whack him in the face. When he covers up, go to the body. Get in as many punches as you can.

❏ Once you have the belt, there are still challenges ahead of you. Use this password to take on another, tougher division of heavyweights: 135 792 4680. Hold down the Select button and press A and B at the same time.

Super Dodge Ball

Manufacturer: *CSG Imagesoft*

Up Front

Dodge ball is played around the world in as many different ways as there are groups of kids. In certain third world villages they play with stones wrapped in leaves—there's no question as to whether you got hit or not. American kids have developed a variation called Army Dodge Ball in which players lose use of a limb when hit. The first time you're hit you have to hold one arm behind your back, the second hit claims your other arm. The third time you are hit you loose a leg and have to hop about in the circle. That's when your older brother tries to hit your good leg while you're in the air.

If dodge ball were an Olympic sport, they would probably play it just as it's played here. Each team consists of six players. The court is a big rectangle divided into two boxes. You have three players inside your box and three players on the outside of the other team's box. The three players outside the other team's box can only throw—they can't be hit.

The three players inside the box are really where the action is. Not only are they the targets, but they can be the most effective offensively when they throw power shots at the other team.

There's only one knock against this game. The graphics will overload at times, and you'll see players half shown on the screen. This is similar to the way the screen flakes out in Double Dribble. Don't let it bother you, though—if you can put up with a little thing like that, you'll find that this game is a whole lot of fun!

To clean up a quote from Gen. George Patton, "The idea of war is not to die for your country, but to make the other guy die for his." This also sums up the idea behind Super Dodge Ball. Each player in the box has a life meter. When the life meter expires, the player becomes an angel and floats off to dodge ball heaven.

Getting Started

Super Dodge Ball is war! Us versus them. And you can choose any of three modes of play:

World Cup	This is the main event for one player. You go to dodge ball war with teams from other countries. If you make it past the Russians, you win the Cup.
Vs.	In this variation you can choose a team and take on a friend in a little friendly war.
Bean Ball	This isn't war, this is chaos! Six players (as many as five can be controlled by the computer) take over a school yard and play Smear. It's every man for himself. The last one standing is the winner.

Each mode comes in three skill levels—easy, normal, and difficult. Before you can master this game, you'll need to learn several controller moves:

⬍◆◆	To walk, push the arrow in the direction you want to go. To run, push the arrow twice in the direction you want to go (usually left or right).
Ⓐ Ⓑ	Press A and B at the same time to jump.
Ⓑ	Throw. While the ball is in the air, use the up and down arrows to make it curve. Some players can throw a curve better than others.
Ⓐ Ⓑ	To pick up a ball from the ground, walk up to it and press either A or B.

Ⓑ   To catch a ball coming toward you, press B.

Ⓐ   To duck a ball coming at you, press A.

Any player in the box can take a power shot. But of course, not all players have the same type of power shot, and not all of them are as effective as others. Each player has slightly different controls to make him take a power shot. You will have to experiment, but most of them require a running jump shot and some kind of action on the arrows at the same time:

Running throw—press an arrow twice to run, then press B to throw before you cross the center line.

Running jump throw—run, jump with A and B, then throw with the B button by itself.

Moving On

In World Cup play you travel around the world taking on team after team. Here is a quick run-down of the teams:

Team	
USA	This is your team in World Cup play—capable of beating any other team on any given day.
All Stars	U.S. professionals—lots of glitz, but weak on defense.
England	Fairly strong. Lots of big guys.
India	It takes a lot of shots to put these guys down.
Iceland	Lots of energy, but not skilled in fundamentals.
China	Easy pickings.
Kenya	Their court is sand, so your guys can't quite crank it up all the way. They have some strong players.
Japan	The third ranked team in the world. Get Fuji if you can.
Russia	Big guys with long life meters. When you play them, you are always the underdog.

In the Vs. mode, you and a friend can pick your favorite teams and go at it.

In both the World Cup and Vs. modes, you can control only one player at a time. The computer controls the other five. To change the player you are controlling, pass the ball to the one you want to control.

Bean Ball is a blast! One or two players can join in. The rest of the players are controlled by the computer. The programming here is excellent because they don't automatically go after you. They will target each other too.

Master Tips

❏ When a player gets down to three bars on his life meter, he gets stunned a bit when he's hit. It will take him a few seconds to recover. This is a good time for one of your outside throwers to target him. Hitting a stunned player with a power shot can be a quick way of getting him out. Hit 'em when they're down!

❏ In Bean Ball, don't run into the sides of the screen when you have the ball or you'll help do yourself in.

❏ When you hit a player with the ball, the number that floats up is a measure of how hard you hit him. Harder shots do more damage.

❏ One way to win the Bean Ball contest is to stay out of the pack when you don't have the ball. Most of the time the computer-controlled player will target a closer opponent. Let them take each other out, then come on aggressively when just one or two are left.

❏ After you defeat the Russians in World Cup play, you can take on your twins by pressing A and B together at just the right time.

Tecmo Bowl

Manufacturer: *Tecmo*

Up Front

Of all the sports simulations available on the Nintendo system, football is probably the hardest to program. With twenty-two players on the field, the screen gets crowded in a hurry. Although baseball comes close with nine players per side, the only time you'll see all eighteen on the field at once is when the benches clear for a fight. Not so with football; each player on the field has something to do with what's going on. For this reason, none of the football simulations rival Bases Loaded II for realism. There just isn't enough programming room to include onside kicks, fake punts, line stunts, double safety blitzes, and a couple of dozen other facets of the game that make it one of the most exciting spectator sports in history.

Having cleared the table of the negatives right away, we should point out that of all the football games we have seen Tecmo Bowl is the leader.

The sideline view is the closest to the way you see NFL games on television, and is close enough to see what each of the major players is doing at the snap of the ball. While play selection is limited (each team has only four basic plays), it's varied enough to keep a trick or two in reserve until the fourth quarter.

Tecmo Bowl offers you twelve pro teams. Since this game is licensed by the Players Association, not the NFL itself, the teams aren't called the Redskins and the Dolphins, but the players on the roster are the real guys who started for those teams when the game was released. Those players' styles have been incorporated as much as possible into the action.

Getting Started

You can play the game in any of three ways. In the one-player mode, you can take on the computer in a simulated season. At the end of each game you get a password that lets you continue the season.

In two-player mode, you pick your team and go head to head with a friend.

Tecmo Bowl has a really strange feature called the Coach mode. In this mode you call the formations, but the computer executes the plays, sort of like the Dallas Cowboys under Tom Landry.

The mechanics of the game are fairly simple. On kicks, you'll see a pulsating meter that determines the strength of the kick. On all other plays, the offense chooses one of four plays and the defense chooses one of four defensive plays.

Each player controls one of the players on the field at a time. When a pass is completed or the defense intercepts the ball, control changes automatically to the runner.

Between plays, a screen shows the offensive playbook. Usually the book contains two running and two passing formations. (True to form, the San Francisco team has three passing and one running formation.) Under each of the plays is a picture of a controller showing which arrow to hold down when you press the A button to lock in your selection.

The defensive player has no visual aid. Pressing the up arrow selects a rush up the middle. The left and right arrows select rushes that cheat in one direction or the other, and the down arrow selects a less aggressive prevent-defense. When the offense comes to the line, the defensive player can select which player to control by pressing button A until his controller number appears over the player's head. The scoreboard at the top of the screen also shows that player's name.

When a receiver catches the ball, you automatically get control of him, and your controller number appears above his head.

Moving On

The controller moves your player differently, depending on whether you're playing offense or defense:

Offense

⬍◀▶	Direct the player's motions.
Ⓐ	Snap the ball.
ⒶⒷ	On pass plays, snap the ball, then press A to change the intended receiver and B to pass.
Ⓐ	On running plays, press A repeatedly to dodge and break tackles.

Defense

Ⓐ   Break free of a block.

Ⓑ   Make a diving tackle.

Master Tips

❏ Study the teams and their plays. Each team has a different personality. Some teams like Chicago and L.A. have good running games, while others like San Francisco and Miami have passing power to spare. Some defenses are better than others. If this all sounds like the NFL, it's supposed to.

❏ The quarterback can run out of the pocket on passing plays—some can run the ball better than others. You cannot, however, pass from a running formation.

❏ Defenders and receivers can run so far that they disappear from the screen. When this happens, they will be marked with triangles on the edge of the screen. Try this—take a defender off to one side of the field and quickly change intended receivers with button A, then throw the bomb. Watch out though, some computerized defensive backs are good enough to make the interception.

❏ When time is running out and you want to prevent the offense from scoring, take a play from the pros. Take control of one of your defensive backs. When the ball is snapped, run back and play center field. This way, any pass will be caught in front of you. Then you can run up and make the tackle.

❏ If you have a fast quarterback, try this trick to make some long completions. Snap the ball and fade way back (twenty or more yards) before throwing the ball. This draws lots of defenders across the line of scrimmage, leaving a deep receiver wide open. It's risky, but if you use it sparingly it works.

Track and Field II

Manufacturer: *Konami*

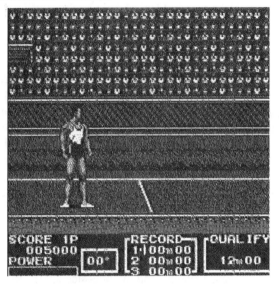

Up Front

In this simulation of track and field events for the NES, Konami has managed to provide much better graphics and a touch more realism than the earlier version of this game.

To be successful at Track and Field II you will have to learn how to control your player in a wide variety of ways in order to bring home the gold. Each event requires a different set of skills, and different timing.

Getting Started

Several play modes are available with this game. The training mode lets you practice each event until you have it down. In the two-player mode you work alone or against a computer opponent. Once you've finished the event, the second player gets a chance.

The Olympic mode is the really tough part of this game. You must endure four days of qualifications in the preliminary rounds, then you have four days of medal rounds. In other words, you must win eight levels to succeed. Each of the days features three of the twelve events. To continue on, you must win all three (or at least get a high qualifying score)—otherwise the game is over. Each day that you survive you get a password that lets you continue from where you left off.

The third play mode is the versus mode where you can take on a friend in head-to-head competition in Fencing, Tae kwon do (tie quan dough), and good old-fashioned arm wrestling.

A lot of these games are easier if you have a controller with a turbo mode. Unfortunately, it can also diminish play value. Some of the events are too easy when you use turbo.

Moving On

Each of the events has a unique set of controller actions and strategies. Here is a quick run-down of each.

Fencing

The left and right arrows are used to move in and out. B is a blocking move. A by itself or with the up or down arrow is a thrusting move. Come in close and block. As the opponent moves away, thrust down and in.

Triple Jump

Punch button A repeatedly and quickly to run as fast as possible. Just before the take-off line, press B and hold it down until you get a number you like in the angle box on the status area of the screen. Try to keep your angle around 55 degrees. When your lead foot touches the ground, press B and hold it again. The third jump is just like the second.

The longer you hold B after the jump, the higher the angle of the jump. Too much angle and you use your energy gaining height. Too little angle and you can't get distance.

Freestyle Swimming

Button A makes you swim, and the B button lets you breathe. Use the down arrow to change swimming strokes.

Keep a good balance of swimming and breathing. When you compete against the computer, watch where his levels are and then experiment with your own settings.

High Diving

Button A will cycle through all the starting stances available until you press B to start the dive. From that point on, use button A with arrow buttons to execute twists and flips. Use up and down to straighten up the entry into the water.

High scores take lots of flips and twists, plus a nice straight entry into the water. It's difficult.

Clay Pigeon Shooting

Press button B to launch the target, the arrow buttons to move the sights, and button A to shoot.

This one takes practice. The farther down range you let a target get, the harder it is to hit. The funny thing about this part of the game is that they don't let you use a light gun. The exhibition portion of the game uses the light gun, so how hard could it be to include it here?

The Hammer Throw

This one will give you blisters! Press the arrow buttons in order counterclockwise to make the thrower begin spinning around. When the thrower begins to flash, press A to throw the hammer.

This is one of those angle deals like the triple jump. The longer you hold down button A, the higher the angle of the throw. Experiment to find the best angle for the speed that you can get the guy spinning.

Tae Kwon Do

This is a lot like most of the kung fu games. If you are good at those, you will be good at this one:

◀▶	Move in and out.
▲	Jump.
▼	Duck.
Ⓐ	Punch.
Ⓑ	With or without arrows, gives you three types of kicking action.

You have three rounds of three minutes each to kick the life out of your opponent. You must reduce his meter to zero before he lowers yours.

Pole Vault

Of all the events, pole vaulting takes the best timing. Run down the track by repeatedly tapping A. Plant the pole with B and hold it down. To release the pole, release B. While in the air, button A helps you assume the correct position for clearing the bar.

You get three tries at each new height. Blow it three times and the event is over.

Canoeing

This event can get positively madcap. Press button A repeatedly to make the boat go forward. Use B the same way to go backward. Left and right arrows steer the nose of the canoe.

You have to thread your way through a series of gates. Gates with blank signs are normal—barrel through them. Gates with a slash mean you have to go through them from the back side. Gates marked with an R mean you have to go through with the back end of the boat first.

Archery

Just as in real archery, this part of the game demands precision. Press A repeatedly to pull back the bow. Use the arrow keys to aim. B launches the arrow.

Watch out for changing wind conditions—they'll affect your shot. As the distance gets longer, increase the angle slightly and pull back harder. Turbo really makes pulling the bow a breeze.

Hurdles

Here is one exception to the computer rule, sort of. When in the two-player mode, you're both on the same track. The third lane is run by the computer. Use the following controls to move:

Ⓐ	Press A repeatedly to run.
Ⓑ	Jump. Hold down B during the upward part of the jump to stay out of the water. Turbo makes this one too darn easy.

Horizontal Bar

Keep button A blazing to keep up your rotation. Watch the power meter. When the power meter is high, hit B to perform some sort of a move. When Finish shows up in the movement box, press B to dismount. Time it right or you'll land on your backside.

Master Tips

❑ In Olympic mode, try hang gliding just for fun. Press A repeatedly to get up speed. Use B to take off. Watch the wind direction meter and the big flat hill to the left. Glide on to the target at the other end of the screen. If you get there at the right speed, you will land automatically. Use B to slow down and A to make a running landing.

❑ In Olympic mode, you can also choose target practice as an exhibition event. You can choose to use the zapper light gun or the controller. Put the sights on the gangsters popping up out of the cars, doors, and manholes, and blast away. What this has to do with track and field is anybody's guess, but there it is. Perhaps mobster massacre will be an Olympic sport someday.

❑ In arm wrestling (which is only available in the Versus mode), press A as fast as you can to exert force against your opponent. If your opponent's power meter smoothly glides to the top, make him turn off turbo mode on his controller—otherwise, you won't have a chance.

Skate or Die

Manufacturer: *Ultra*

Up Front

It's the rad fad, shredding asphalt against the likes of Rodney Recloose and his weirded-out kid, Bionic Lester, not to mention Pete and Eddie. Who are these punked out skateboard freaks who make Road Warriors look like a Disney film? They are the cast and crew of Skate or Die. While the characters in this game are strange, the game itself is a real challenge and more than a little fun. There are five different skateboard events in all:

High Jump	High Jump takes place in the U-Zone, a trough-shaped ramp setup. You compete to see who can come up out of the trough the farthest.
Freestyle	In Freestyle, you're still in the U-Zone, but now you perform tricks for points.
Downhill	The Downhill event is a race to the finish line where you can abandon the high road for shortcut jumps and the tube.
Joust	In Joust, two riders take to a drained out swimming pool and battle it out with a boffing stick. Each rider takes the stick for five passes through the pool and tries to knock the other off his board.
Jam	In Jam, you ride through the back alleys in a race to the street. To win, you kick and punch your opponent off his board so you can get ahead.

Getting Started

To begin the game, press Start—you're now inside Rad Rodney's Flesh 'n' Asphalt Skateboard Shoppe. Use the arrow keys to move the words *Skate or Die* around the screen. As you move the cursor around the screen, Rodney has some words for you. You may choose one of four options: view high scores, take practice, sign in, and compete. To compete, you must sign in first, so Rodney will know where to send the body or where to put you on the high score list. Up to eight players can sign in and compete against each other.

If you want to practice (and you should), choose the practice mode. In this mode, you can try any of the events as many times as you like until you get the hang of it. The practice mode is an important feature of this game, as each event uses slightly different controller moves—it takes a while to get the hang of things. The competition mode takes you through the same runs, but each run is separate and the high scores go into the trophy display. High scores are erased when you reset the cartridge or turn off the power.

Moving On

Since this game consists of a variety of competitions, let's look at each competition in turn.

The Downhill

The Downhill race is timed—you earn points based on the time it takes you to get down the hill. Radical moves and certain jumps will also shave time off the run and earn you bonus points.

You can choose either of two modes here—Regular foot and Goofy foot. In the regular race, you control the rider from the perspective of seeing him on the screen. In the Goofy race, the perspective is reversed, as if you yourself were on the board. Use the following controls to make your moves:

◀▶	Make slow turns.
Ⓑ	Use the arrows and button B together to make quick, radical turns.
Ⓐ	Use the up arrow and button A to jump. Use the down arrow and button A to duck into the tunnel. If you take a spill, press A to get back up and try again.

Freestyle

The Freestyle competition takes place in the U-Zone. You get ten passes through the trough, five from each side. The trick is to perform aerial maneuvers as you pop up out of the trough. Use the following controls to make your moves:

Ⓐ	Press button A continuously to build up speed in the trough (turbo really helps). If you don't press any other buttons, this results in a low jump.

◀▶	Perform a Kickturn or Rock n' Roll maneuver (depending on what direction you're going).
Ⓐ◀▶	Hold down the left or right arrow button and press A once to perform a Foot Plant or Rail side.
◀▶ ⒶⒶ	Hold down the left or right arrow button and press A twice to perform a Hand Plant or Ollie.
Ⓐ	Press A once (no arrow) to perform a medium jump.
ⒶⒶ	Press A twice (no arrow) to perform a high jump.

High Jump

To get the best marks in the High Jump, press button A to get started. Gain speed with B (turbo is almost essential here, unless you have the fastest trigger finger west of the Pecos). At the point of your jump, press A, and press A again at the top of your jump.

The Jam

The Jam is one of the wildest races you will ever take part in. Use the controller just as you did in Downhill. Along the way, you will want to smash, trash, and bash your opponent for bonus points. Add the following maneuvers to your Downhill moves:

Ⓑ◀▶	Press B and the arrow in the direction the skater is facing to punch your opponent.
▲◀▶	Press the up arrow and either left or right arrow to perform a high kick.
◀▶	Press either the left or right arrow to perform a medium kick.
▼◀▶	Press the down arrow and either the left or right arrow to perform a low kick.

The more you abuse your opponent, the slower he will be and the more bonus points you will earn.

Joust

Joust is one of the most fun events in the game. You and an opponent (you can take your pick of three computer opponents) take turns wielding the boff stick for five passes through the drained out pool. The object is to knock the other guy off his board to score a point.

After a score or after five passes, the stick goes to the other rider and you go on defense. The idea on defense is to avoid being knocked off the board. The first player to get a three-point advantage is the winner. If the round ends without a winner, the play is extended and the first rider to take a two-point lead is the winner.

Master Tips

❏ Speed and stunts give you the most bonus points in Downhill. Taking the Death Ramp, ducking through the drain pipe, and jumping the little walkways add bonus points fast.

❏ In Downhill, you can earn extra bonus points if you don't swing out and then turn left to cross the finish. Simply jump the grass that sticks out there and cross the finish line coming straight down the screen. Really rad, dude!

❏ The more punches and kicks you can get in on your opponent in the Jam, the higher your point score. Also, don't take the obvious path. Bonus points are won by taking unique paths as well.

❏ Scoring well in Freestyle and High Jump definitely takes a turbo controller. You can actually get so high out of the trough that a fall will put you right through the plywood. Gnarley, man.

❏ You'll do better in the Joust on defense if you and your opponent aren't synchronized. Try to hit the top of the wall at a different time than the other guy.

❏ In Joust, Pete's kind of tough, Eddie's the next toughest, and Lester is the hardest of the bunch.

HOT CONTROLLERS

A wide variety of specialized controllers are available that provide you with hardware power-ups like turbo fire, slow motion, and hands-free operation. These products range from simple joysticks to motion-sensing controllers that you don't even have to touch.

The products below represent only a small fraction of the products available. We selected these products because they represent the variety of products available—we're not recommending that you limit yourself to the products listed here.

Hot
Controllers

Nintendo Controllers

Nintendo itself markets several controllers that are meant to replace the standard controllers that come with the NES. These controllers tend to set the standards for features found on those from other manufacturers. That is the only reason they are presented first.

Hands Free Controller

Nintendo engineers worked with players at the Seattle Children's Hospital to come up with a controller that gives quadriplegic players access to the Nintendo system.

The unit is strapped to the player's chest. The player moves a joystick with his or her chin, and sips and puffs on a straw to work buttons A and B. The HFC can actually help patients strengthen their jaw and neck muscles.

Nintendo is handling this item on a non-profit basis. The cost is $120.00. For an extra fifty dollars, they will even include the control deck. For more information call 1-800-422-2602.

NES Advantage

If you are one of those players who gets exited and begins squeezing the controller until your hands hurt, a joystick may be the answer. The NES Advantage is the granddaddy of NES joysticks.

This unit puts a short joystick on a big, heavy base, then adds oversized A and B buttons placed on an angle that just fits how your arm bends when it's on a table. Add variable speed turbo, slow motion capability, and a switch that lets you go from player one to player two, and you have a good, rugged, all-around controller.

NES Max

The Max is the Advantage's little brother. This controller has a handlebar shape and a big round button in place of the arrow buttons. This makes it easier to make diagonal moves by pressing down and left (for example) at the same time. On the Max, you simply press the spot midway between the two directions.

Two buttons that sit just below the A and B buttons let you turn on turbo fire. These buttons make this controller a simple but effective power-up.

NES Satellite

Other manufacturers came out with wireless controllers before Nintendo, but this one is a wireless with a twist. All of the other wireless units make you use a new controller. The Satellite lets you plug your favorite controller into the unit; it then transmits that controller's signals to the receiver by way of infrared light. This is the same type of system that the remote control for a VCR uses.

The NES Satellite has one other advantage—up to four players can plug in. This is the only way to take full advantage of some of the newer games like Super Spike V-Ball where four players can actually compete at the same time.

Camerica Controllers

Camerica produces an entire line of replacement controllers. Their Freedom Pad is a wireless remote that features a round button for the arrows like the Nintendo Max, but has the control cross-raised on the button. This controller also has two-speed turbo.

The Freedom Stick is a wireless version of the Advantage, but lacks slow motion. The turbo is not variable. They also make a wireless model that has A and B buttons on both sides of the joystick. This makes it easier for left-handed players.

Toycard SSS

Hudson Soft (Bomberman and Dino Riki) markets a replacement controller that is extremely popular with parents. Let's face it, the music and sound effects on a lot of games can be downright irritating with their repetition. Players don't notice it so much because they're immersed in the action.

The Toycard controller solves this problem. This controller has a short cord that plugs into the NES Control Deck's audio output jack. Miniature earplugs connect to the bottom of the controller so the player can hear the game sounds, but the TV sound can be turned down so other members of the family aren't bothered.

There is a volume control above the arrow buttons, and the sound in the headphones shifts when you press the arrows. When your character moves to the left, so does the sound. If this annoys you, there is a switch to turn the added sound effects off.

Two-speed turbo rounds out the features of this well-made controller.

Power Glove

This is one of the truly unique hardware power-ups available for the NES. The Power Glove uses an L-shaped bar draped over the TV set. The bar contains three motion detectors to sense where the glove is. The glove itself has a shell that straps to your wrist. Two ultrasonic transmitters are mounted on the shell just above the knuckles. These transmitters tell the sensors where the glove is and what it's doing.

In addition to the regular controller buttons, the Power Glove has another group of buttons that programs how the NES responds to the glove's moves.

This power-up takes a lot of getting used to. Unlike the controllers previously mentioned, this hardware power-up introduces a whole new dimension to playing games. To punch your way through Mike Tyson's Punch Out, you actually make punching movements. At first it may seem awkward and hard to control, but soon you will feel quite comfortable with the Power Glove.

It is a lot of fun pressing the A button simply by bending your thumb. It has a real Darth Vader kind of feel to it. Add slow motion and multi-level turbo and you have a lot of excitement in the palm of your hand.

U-Force

The U-Force is unique because it is the only controller that lets you play the NES without touching anything! You don't wear gloves or put radioactive paint on your fingers. Instead you move your hands and fingers within a force field to tell the controller what signals to send to the NES.

The U-Force is a plastic case that folds like a clamshell for carrying and storage. Inside the case are ultrasonic sensors that detect the movements of your hands and translate them into controller signals. This leaves you free to create hand gestures (like grasping an imaginary steering wheel or punching) to control the game action.

There are switches on the U-force that change how the unit responds to your movements, so you can use the U-Force with a wide selection of games.

The U-Force comes with T-shaped handgrips that you can insert into a socket on the bottom sensor board. The handgrips let you practice things like steering maneuvers with something in your hands. Once you have become comfortable with the feel of the T-bar, try using the same motions with nothing in your hands to control the game.

Double Player

Acclaim Entertainment offers the Double Player—a set of two wireless controllers that feature the rounded control cross, turbo fire, and slow motion.

Zoomer

Beeshu makes a wide variety of joysticks and controllers, but the Zoomer is designed especially for those players who take flying and driving games seriously.

The Beeshu Zoomer (say that three times real fast) is a U-shaped steering wheel with firing buttons at the top of the handles. This controller adds realism and excitement to driving and flying games. For something completely different, try using the Zoomer on different types of games.

The Zoomer features turbo fire and slow motion along with its unique layout.

GAMEBOY

Nintendo's latest entry into the game market is GameBoy. This small, hand-held game system has captured the fancy of millions of players since its introduction late in 1989.

GameBoy

by Allen Wyatt

The Up Side

Manufacturer: *Nintendo*

GameBoy's popularity is due to several of the advanced features it offers:

- ❏ Small, compact design. You can hold the GameBoy comfortably in one hand, although you'll want to use both hands for playing games.

- ❏ An impressive dot-matrix display. Details are surprisingly visible on the GameBoy's screen.

- ❏ Stereo sound. Depending on how a game was programmed, the sound from a GameBoy can be quite impressive. A volume control and headphones are provided so you don't drive those around you crazy.

- ❏ Comes with one game cartridge (Tetris). Talk about addicting! What a game to start off with—and it's included at no additional cost.

- ❏ Two-player option. You and a friend can play the same game simply by connecting your GameBoys with the cable that's provided. Each of you, of course, must be using the same game cartridge.

- ❏ Take-along portability. GameBoy is small enough to travel with you just about anywhere.

The Down Side

On the other side of the fence, the GameBoy has a few draw-backs, including:

- ❏ Incompatible games. Your favorite Nintendo games (which you purchased for your Nintendo system) will not work with GameBoy. You will have to buy all new games.

- ❏ Two GameBoys (and game cartridges) are required for two-player mode. While this is also an advantage, it doubles the amount of money you must spend for two-player action.

- ❏ Black-and-white screen. The colorful displays of a Nintendo game are reduced to black and white for the GameBoy. If you really enjoy full color, you may find the GameBoy disappointing.

- ❏ Battery life. You can only play as long as your batteries last. If you are an avid player, you can go through a set of 4 AA batteries in less than a day.

GameBoy Tip: To reduce your long-term costs, buy and use rechargeable batteries. Keep a set in your GameBoy and another in the recharger. That way you won't go broke. Another option is to buy the GameBoy AC adapter, as described later in this chapter. The only problem is that this requires you to be near an electrical plug (obviously not practical when using your GameBoy in the car).

In addition, some players, already comfortable with the familiar dimensions of a full-size Nintendo screen, have complained that they dislike the narrow GameBoy screen. Although it's true that you get less horizontal viewing area for the GameBoy, you can quickly overcome this limitation with a little practice.

The Controls

The controls on the GameBoy are similar to the controls on the Nintendo game controllers. There's a small joystick control on the left side of the GameBoy, A and B control buttons on the right side, and the Select and Start switches near the bottom. The joystick lets you move up, down, left, and right; the purpose of the A and B buttons depends on the game you're playing. Select is usually used for selecting game options, and Start is used to start or pause a game.

Besides the ever-important game controls, the GameBoy has two dials that you'll use pretty often. On the left side of the game unit is the contrast control. Use this control to adjust the darkness of GameBoy's picture to a comfortable level.

On the opposite (right) side of the game unit is the volume control. You can adjust this as necessary to please yourself or others around you. If you want it loud, but you're getting strange looks from Mom and Dad who are trying to watch TV, you can use the earplugs. Connect these to the bottom of the GameBoy, and the quality of the stereo system will really come through.

The Video Link Cable

GameBoy comes with a special 5-foot video link cable. What good is it? This cable allows you to connect your GameBoy with another GameBoy for fast-action two-player games.

GameBoy Tip: Make sure your GameBoy is turned off before connecting the video link cable. This protects the electronics inside the GameBoy from accidents.

The video link cable plugs into each GameBoy on the upper right side of the unit. This connector is right above the volume dial.

The next place where you plug in the video link cable is marked EXT. CONNECTOR. You must remove the small plastic plug that's covering the connector—this is easy to do (if you have to force it, then you're not doing it right).

GameBoy Tip: Don't lose the plastic plug that covers the video link connector on the GameBoy. You'll need it later when you go back to playing by yourself. Put it somewhere safe, or store it in an unused plastic game box until needed.

Now simply plug one end of the video link cable into this connector and the other into another GameBoy. Both ends of the cable are the same—there's no "correct end" to keep track of. Now you and another player can play against each other. Both of you must have the same game cartridge in your Game-Boys, and you must turn on both machines at the same time.

Only a few of the currently available GameBoy games work for two players. In the next section that lists the available games we've included special notations to indicate if a game can be played by two players.

GameBoy Options

Because the GameBoy is a self-contained system designed to go with you anywhere, the game includes very few options as of this writing. One option you may find helpful, however, is a carrying case—there are a number on the market. Nintendo offers a case that allows you to carry your GameBoy on your belt. Nuby offers one that is harder and allows you to store all your GameBoy pieces (including up to six games) in one location.

Another option you may find valuable is the AC adapter that Nintendo offers. This option, while initially expensive ($27.95), saves you money on batteries. Of course, it won't save you much if you're playing on the road.

Rumor has it that other GameBoy options will be available in the near future, including an option that lets you hook your GameBoy up to your television. If this is true, you could then add a new dimension to your GameBoy and overcome the drawback of the small screen.

The Games

While the current selection of games for the GameBoy does not yet approach that of the Nintendo game system, games are available for all tastes. And new games are being added every day. Every time I visit my local game dealer I find another game tempting me to give it a try.

GameBoy Tip: When switching game cartridges, make sure the GameBoy is turned off. Inserting a game cartridge with the GameBoy turned on could damage either the Game-Boy or the cartridge.

GameBoy Tip: When you're not playing your games, put them in their plastic boxes for storage. This will protect them from dust, dirt, and water, and from your little brother.

The following sections take a quick look at many of the games available for GameBoy, but don't expect a complete list. By the time this book reaches the bookstores, there will probably be a half dozen new games on the shelves.

Alleyway

Manufacturer: *Nintendo*

Alleyway is a spin-off of one of the oldest video games around—Breakout. You use your joystick to control a paddle at the bottom of the screen. When you press button A, a ball is released which you must deflect with the paddle. As the ball bounces off your paddle, it moves up and hits a group of blocks (or bricks) which disappear as they're hit.

In this variation, you become Mario, and enter the paddle to control it from inside. There are four levels, each consisting of blocks which are arranged differently or behave differently.

Level 1 has standard blocks; the 84 blocks (7 rows of 12 blocks each) are stationary. You can chip away at the blocks from the bottom, or you can guide the ball up either the left or right side to remove a lot of blocks from the top of the wall. This is the best way to rack up lots of points.

Level 2 has the same number of blocks as level 1, except that they scroll across the screen from right to left. You still have the open slot where you can slip the ball above the wall to collect lots of points, but it's harder to hit because it's a moving target.

Level 3 starts out innocently enough—it looks just like level 1. But after playing for a while, you'll notice that the blocks start moving down toward you. Work fast to remove all the blocks in time.

Level 4 is a bonus level. The blocks are in the shape of Mario (you have more blocks in this level), and the ball moves faster than in the other levels. Also, at this level your paddle becomes shorter after a deflected ball hits the top of the screen.

After you complete level 4, the series of screens starts over again, as with level 1.

Baseball (Two Players)

Manufacturer: *Nintendo*

The summer classic falls into the palm of your hand in this full-featured game. You can almost hear the roar of the crowd and taste the peanuts and CrackerJack. You control the team line-ups as you play against the GameBoy or against another player through the video link.

Another interesting feature of this game is that you can select either the USA mode or the Japan mode. The modes are identical, except the player names reflect the nation you select. You can then pick whether you want the beginner's mode. This mode plays a little slower, and you get music throughout the game.

This version of baseball is not as full-featured as other baseball games on the Nintendo system, but you can still have fun. When you are at bat, you control when the batter swings and where he stands in relation to the plate. When you're in the field, you control where the pitcher stands and when he pitches. The fielders (for both teams) sort of do their own thing—you can't control their actions.

The Castlevania Adventure

Manufacturer: *Konami*

Simon is back in this all-time favorite, searching for Count Dracula to put an end to his blood-thirsty career. As Simon, you must maneuver your way across the countryside and through four dangerous levels, defeating various monsters and avoiding deadly traps. You gain strength from using your whip to gather candles, hearts, crystals, and other magical tokens along the way.

Your quest is to rid the land of the monsters and any enemies which may crop up in your path. Your ultimate goal is to face Count Dracula at the end of level 4 and eliminate him before he gets you. Be quick in your journey, however, because each level has a time limit. When your time is up, your life is over.

MotoCross Maniacs (Two Players)

Manufacturer: *Ultra Software*

You're behind the handlebars, blazing your way into history as a MotoCross Maniac. You must learn to control your bike through many challenging courses as you rack up points based on your speed and savvy. As you race against the clock, you must race over ramps, hurdle jumps, and complete challenging loop-the-loops. You can even use nitro to increase the pace of the game.

You can ride solo, play against the GameBoy, or play two-player mode through the video link. If you're playing against the computer, you still must try for the best time possible. But if you're connected with another player, watch out! First across the line wins—no holds barred.

Choose from eight courses and up to three levels of difficulty. Each course has a time limit. And even though you may seem indestructible, rising from each crash to ride again, you lose valuable time with each spill. Remember, you're out to beat the clock.

Revenge of the 'Gator (Two Players)

Manufacturer: *Nintendo*

If you like pinball, this game is for you. Revenge of the 'Gator is an elaborate pinball game, with four regular levels and three bonus levels. While the pinball is still moving, you can switch from one screen to another. You have to play for a while to get the hang of how the screens progress.

Revenge of the 'Gator has some of the best stereo sound effects of the games I have played. It certainly has the most innovative title screen I've seen. Don't be too quick to press the Start key—before long, you will be entertained by dancing alligators. Overall, this game will bring you hours of challenging play.

Super Mario Land

Manufacturer: *Nintendo*

This is a variation on the ever-popular Super Mario Brothers. You may already be familiar with this game from your full-size Nintendo system.

In this version, you are Mario and are on a quest to save Princess Daisy amid the traps and pitfalls of ancient Egypt. You must fight winged demons and other monsters, avoid falling ceilings, and jump over many obstacles to rescue the fair maiden. In fact, over 25 different creatures are there to harass you in your journey.

As you rush to find the princess, make sure you explore every avenue and take advantage of the power-up flowers, invincibility stars, and magic mushrooms. Don't dawdle, however. There is a time limit on each level, and you must beware of false princesses and other traps not easily visible.

Tennis (Two Players)

Manufacturer: *Nintendo*

As you play against the GameBoy or another player through the video link, you must be fast on your feet and work the entire court to win. You control the serves and your returns to outwit your opponent.

If you're playing against another player using the video link cable, both players view the game from their own side of the court. This two-player version can present the most challenging form of tennis.

Tetris (Two Players)

Manufacturer: *Nintendo*

This game comes with the GameBoy. It is an adaptation of the popular full-size game which has been available on Nintendo and personal computer systems for years. The object of the game is to move and turn falling shapes, guiding them so that they come rest without any gaps between pieces. As you complete rows, the rows disappear and you receive points. The number of points you receive depends on how many rows you complete with each game piece you add. You get the most points for completing a tetris—four rows at once.

In the two-player version, if you complete at least two lines at once, they disappear from your screen and appear on your opponent's screen. This frustrating twist leads to hours of addicting, challenging play.

AIR FORTRESS

16 challenging levels of video game play

- Battle enemy forces on the Air Base, picking up energy and weapons!
- Into the Air Fortress, to search out and destroy the Central Reactor!
- Find your way back to your ship before the Air Fortress self-destructs!

Official Nintendo Seal of Quality

Licensed by Nintendo for play on the

Nintendo
ENTERTAINMENT SYSTEM®

Danger around every bend in the Air Fortress!

High-speed arcade action on the Air Base!

HAL AMERICA INC.
The Funatic Specialists